Chadwick Library Edition

*

Selected Written Works of Rudolf Steiner

Vol. 3

MYSTICS AT THE DAWN OF THE MODERN AGE

AND THEIR RELATION TO THE CURRENT NATURAL-SCIENTIFIC PARADIGM

RUDOLF STEINER

MYSTICS AT THE DAWN OF THE MODERN AGE

AND THEIR RELATION TO THE CURRENT NATURAL-SCIENTIFIC PARADIGM

Translated by
KARL E. ZIMMER
with revisions by JON MCALICE
and THOMAS O'KEEFE

CHADWICK LIBRARY EDITION

Great Barrington, Massachusetts

2017

COPYRIGHT INFORMATION

Chadwick Library Edition is an imprint of
SteinerBooks (Anthroposophic Press)
610 Main Street, Great Barrington, MA 01230 USA
www.steinerbooks.org

Translation by Karl E. Zimmer, with revisions by
Jon McAlice and Thomas O'Keefe.

This book comprises volume 7 in the Collected
Works (CW) of Rudolf Steiner. It is a translation of
Die Mystik im Aufgange des neuzeitlichen Geisteslebens und ihr Verhältnis zur modernen Weltanschauung, published by
Rudolf Steiner Verlag, Dornach, Switzerland, 1987.

ISBN 978-0996921 1-4-5 (Trade Edition)
978-0996921 1-5-2 (Limited Edition)

Printed in Verona, Italy

TABLE OF CONTENTS
Vol. 3

PREFACE TO THE FIRST EDITION
1901

This work discusses the content of my lectures given at the theosophical library in Berlin last winter. Count and Countess Brockdorff invited me to speak on mysticism to an audience who considered such matters vitally important. Ten years ago, I would not have dared agree to such a request. This does not imply that the world of ideas I express today was not alive in me then. This world of ideas is, in fact, fully contained in my *Philosophy of Spiritual Activity*, written in 1894.[1] But to express this world of ideas as I do today and to make it the basis of a discussion, as I did in this work, requires something more than an unshakable conviction of its conceptual truth. It requires an intimate familiarity with these ideas, which is gained only through many years of life. Only now, after having gained this familiarity, do I dare to speak as one will perceive in this work.

Whoever does not enter into my world of ideas in an *unprejudiced way* will discover in it contradiction upon contradiction. I recently dedicated a book on nineteenth-century philosophy (Berlin, 1900)[2] to the great scientist Ernst Haeckel, and brought the book to an end with a justification of his world of thoughts. In the following expositions, I speak with fully assenting devotion concerning the mystics, from Meister Eckhart to Angelus Silesius. Concerning other "contradictions" that one or another has brought against me, I would rather not even mention them here. I am not surprised when one faction accuses me of being a "mystic" and another of being a "materialist." If I find that the Jesuit priest Müller has solved a difficult chemical problem, and if I happen to agree with him without qualification *in this particular matter*, then one certainly could not accuse me of being an adherent of Jesuitism without being deemed a fool by those with understanding.

Whoever goes his own way, as I do, must accept many misunderstandings. Basically, they are not difficult to bear. Most such misunderstandings become self-evident once the outlook of one's critics is brought to mind. It is not without humor that I recall the many "critical" judgments leveled at me during my career as a writer. In the beginning, it all went smoothly; I wrote about Goethe and related subjects. Many people felt that they could fit what I had to say into their preconceived notions by saying, "We can honestly characterize works such as Rudolf Steiner's introductions to Goethe's scientific writings as the best writings on this matter."

Later, by the time I had published an independent work, I had become a good deal stupider. Now a benevolent critic offered this advice: "Before he continues on his path as a reformer and publishes his *Philosophy of Spiritual Activity*, one must urgently advise that he first come to an understanding of those two philosophers [Hume and Kant]."[3] Unfortunately, that critic knows only what he has been able to understand from Kant and Hume; he is really advising me to see only what he sees in those thinkers. Once I have accomplished that, he will find me satisfactory. When *The Philosophy of Spiritual Activity* was published, I was judged as though I were the most empty-headed novice. I happened to receive this judgment from a gentleman who needs no other prompting to write books than the fact that he has failed to understand what many others have written. He thoughtfully informed me that I would have noticed my mistakes if I "had pursued my studies of psychology, logic, and epistemology more deeply." And he immediately lists for me all the books I should read to become as smart as he – "Mill, Sigwart, Wundt, Riehl, Paulsen, B. Erdmane."

Especially delightful for me was the advice of a man who is so impressed with his own "understanding" of Kant that he cannot imagine that someone has *read* Kant and yet does not share his opinion. Consequently, he pointed out to me the relevant chapters in Kant's writings that might help me to understand Kant as profoundly as he does.

I have here presented a few *typical* judgments of my world of ideas. Although in themselves they are insignificant, they nevertheless appear to me well-suited to point out, in a symptomatic sense, certain facts that now constitute serious obstacles in the path of those who are engaged with the more advanced questions of cognition. I must follow my own path regardless of the good advice I am given about reading Kant or accusations of heresy because I agree with Haeckel. Therefore, I have written about mysticism without being concerned about the judgments of a devout materialist. To avoid wasting any printer's ink, I would like simply to inform those who might advise me now to read Haeckel's *Riddle of the Universe*[4] that in the last months I have presented about thirty lectures on the book.

I hope I have shown in my work that one can be a faithful follower of the scientific worldview and still seek out the paths *to the soul* that are opened through a *properly understood* mysticism. I go even further and assert that only one who understands spirit in the sense of *true* mysticism can fully understand the reality of nature. One must only beware of confusing true mysticism with the "mystical endeavors" of nebulous minds. I have shown how mysticism can err in chapter VIII of my *Philosophy of Spiritual Activity.*

Rudolf Steiner
Berlin, September 1901

INTRODUCTION

There are magic formulas that have been present in ever new ways throughout the history of ideas. In Greece, one such formula was considered to be an oracle of Apollo. It is: "Know thyself." Such phrases seem to harbor infinite life. They may be encountered along the most diverse paths of spiritual life. As one progresses and becomes able to understand things more deeply, the meaning of such formulas becomes deeper. At times, during our contemplations, they flash like lightning, illuminating our whole inner life. In such moments we almost feel as though we can sense the heartbeat of human evolution. How close we feel to figures from the past when one of their sayings awakens in us the feeling that they too have known such moments! One then feels that one has entered into an intimate relationship with those individuals. One becomes intimately acquainted with Hegel, for example, upon encountering these words from the third volume of his *Lectures on the History of Philosophy*:

> One might say that such things are the abstractions we behold when, in our studies, we allow philosophers to dispute and quarrel and decide matters one way or another; they are abstractions made of mere words. No! Absolutely not! They are acts of universal spirit and, consequently, of fate. In this way, the philosophers are closer to

> the Lord than are those who feed on crumbs of the spirit. They read or write the orders from on high in the original – it is their function to take part in writing them. The philosophers are the mystics who were present at the act in the innermost sanctuary and who participated in it.[5]

When Hegel said this, he experienced one of those moments I described. He had reached the end of his historical analysis of Greek philosophy when he made these statements. Here he showed that the meaning of Neoplatonic wisdom (which he speaks of at this point) had been illuminated in him like a stroke of lightning. At the moment of that illumination, he had become intimately close to spirits such as Plotinus and Proclus. And we become intimately close to him as we read his words.

We also become intimate with the solitary, meditating vicar in Zschopau, Germany, M. Valentinus Wigelius (Valentin Weigel), when we read his words from his 1578 booklet *Know Thyself*:[6]

> We read in the works of old sages the useful proverb *know thyself*, used primarily in reference to worldly behavior – for example, "Look well at yourself, at what you are"; "Examine your heart"; and "Judge yourself, do not censure others." Although, as I say, it is used in human life with respect to behavior, nevertheless the saying *know thyself* may be well-applied to both a natural and a supernatural understanding of humanity. A person should not only look at himself and think

of how he should act toward others, but also understand his inner and outer nature in spirit and in nature – whence he has come, of what he is made, and for what he is intended.

Having taken his own path, Valentin Weigel thus arrived at insights that were summed up for him in the oracle of Apollo.

A similar road to understanding, and the same position with respect to the maxim *know thyself*, can be ascribed to a succession of profound thinkers, beginning with Meister Eckhart (1250–1327) and ending with Angelus Silesius (1624–1677) – a group to which Valentin Weigel also belongs. Common to these thinkers is a strong feeling that in human self-knowledge, a sun rises, illuminating something entirely different from the incidental, individual personality of the beholder. What Spinoza realized in the ethereal height of pure thought – that "the human soul has sufficient knowledge of the eternal, infinite nature of God"[7] – was something they sensed directly. For them, self-knowledge was the path to this eternal and infinite nature. It was clear to them that self-knowledge, in its true form, endows human beings with a new faculty that opens to them a world for which they would otherwise be blind.

It would be difficult to find a better description of the importance of this new faculty than that given by J. G. Fichte in his 1813 Berlin lectures:

Imagine a world of people who are born blind and know only the objects and conditions that

> exist through touch. Go to them and speak of colors and other conditions that exist only for our eyes via the medium of light. Either what you say to them will mean nothing – and it is better if they say so, because in this way you will soon see your mistake, and if you cannot open their eyes it will end such useless talk. – Or, if on some ground or other they indeed wish to give meaning to your teaching, they would be able to understand it only through what has become known to them via touch. They will want to *feel* the light, colors, and other visible qualities; they will believe that they feel them and, within the realm of touch, will invent something they name *color* and deceive themselves with it. They will then misunderstand, distort, and misinterpret.[8]

One could say something similar about what is striven for by the individuals discussed in this book. They viewed self-knowledge as the development of a new faculty. In their understanding, this faculty leads to insights that do not exist for those who do not perceive in the nature of self-knowledge what differentiates it from all other kinds of knowing. Whoever has yet to develop this faculty believes that self-knowledge comes about in a manner similar to knowledge attained through the bodily senses or some other external means. He believes: "Knowledge is knowledge." In the one case, however, the object is in the outer world, and, in the other, the object is our own soul. They hear only words – or at best, abstract thoughts – where those who look more deeply see the essence of inner life: namely, in the dictum that the object is outside ourselves for all other kinds of knowing, whereas in self-knowledge we stand within the object; that all other objects come to us already completed, whereas within our self we actively, creatively weave what we observe.

This explanation may seem to be mere words, even trivial; but when understood properly, it can appear as a higher light that illuminates all other knowledge in a new way. Those who see this explanation as mere words are in the same position as the blind, to whom one might say, "Over there is a bright object." Such a person hears the words, but for this person the brightness is nonexistent. One can gather in oneself all the knowledge of a certain time; but if one fails to perceive the significance of self-knowledge, all knowledge is blind in the higher sense.

The outer world, although independent of us, comes to life within us because it speaks of itself to our spirit. What it tells us must be expressed in a language we understand. A book would be meaningless for us if its contents were presented in an unknown language. In the same way, the world would be meaningless for us if it did not speak to us in our own language. We hear the same language that reaches us from the world of things also from within ourselves. Then, however, it is *indeed* we ourselves who are speaking. It is only a matter of listening properly to the transformation that occurs when we close our perception to external things and listen only to that which sounds from within us. It is precisely for this listening that the new faculty is necessary. If it is not awakened, we tend to believe that what we receive as communications about ourselves are of the same nature as those we receive concerning things outside us; we think there is something concealed that speaks to us as external objects do. If we have the new faculty, then we know that its perceptions are essentially different from those that refer to external objects. Then we know that this faculty does not remain separate from that which it perceives – as the eye remains separate from the object it sees – but that it can completely incorporate the object within itself. If I see an object, the object remains outside me; if I perceive myself, I enter into my own perception. Whoever still seeks for some part of his self outside of what is perceived shows that the actual content of the perception has not been illuminated for him. Johannes Tauler (1300–1361) aptly expressed this truth: *If I were a king and did not know it, I would not be a king.*[9] If I do not become illuminated to myself through self-perception, then I do not exist for myself. But if I become illuminated to myself, then I *possess* myself, through perception, in my most fundamental individual essence. No part of me remains outside of my perception. With the following words, J. G. Fichte strongly points to the difference between self-perception and all other kinds of perception:

> It would be easier to convince most people to consider themselves a piece of lava on the moon than an *'I.'* He who is not united with his self in this sense will not understand any comprehensive philosophy, nor does he need one. Nature, whose machine he is, will lead him without his participation in everything he must do. To philosophize, one must be independent, and independence can be given only by one's own self. We should not want to see without eyes, but neither should we assert that it is only the eye that sees.[10]

The perception of oneself, therefore, is at the same time the *awakening* of the self. Through knowing, we connect the nature of an object with our own nature. What the things of the outer world convey to us in a language we can understand becomes a part of our own self. What comes to meet me is no longer separate from me if I am able to recognize it. Whatever aspects of it I am able to assimilate are incorporated into my own nature. When I awaken my own self, when I perceive what is within me, I also awaken to a higher existence all that I have incorporated into my nature from outside. The light that falls upon me as I awaken also falls upon those things of the world that I have assimilated. A light flares up within me, illuminating me, and, with me, everything I know of the world. All that I know would remain blind knowledge if not for this light falling upon it. I could gain knowledge of everything in the world, but it would not be what it must become within me if this knowledge were not awakened to a higher existence in my being.

What I add to things through this awakening is not a new idea, not something that enriches the breadth of my knowledge. Rather, what I add is something that raises knowledge to a higher level in which everything is endowed with a new brilliance. As long as I do not raise my cognition to this level, then in the higher sense, all knowledge remains worthless to me. The things do exist without me. They harbor their own being within. What significance does it have when I connect another spiritual existence, which recreates things within me, to the existence of what remains outside me? If it were merely a matter of repetition, then it would be pointless to carry this out. But it is a matter of mere repetition only as long as I do not awaken the spiritual essence of what I take into myself to a higher existence within me. If this happens, then I have not merely reproduced the nature of something outer within me, but I have caused it to be reborn on a higher level.

With the awakening of my self, a spiritual *rebirth* of the things of the world takes place. In that rebirth, things manifest qualities that they had not possessed previously. There, outside, is a tree. I take it into my mind. I shine my inner light on what I have apprehended. Within me, the tree becomes more than it is externally. The part of it that enters through the portal of the senses is now received into a spiritual content; an ideal counterpart of the tree is within me. This says infinitely more about the tree than the external tree can tell me. The light that shines from me first reveals to the tree the nature of its being. The tree is now no longer the isolated being that it is by virtue of existing in external space. It becomes a part of the whole spiritual world that lives within me. It combines its meaning with the other ideas that live in me. It becomes a part of the whole organism of ideas that embraces the plant world; it is further integrated into the evolutionary progression of all life.

I could cite another example. Imagine that I throw a stone horizontally. It moves in an arched path and, eventually, falls to the ground. In successive moments I see it at different locations. After some reflection, I arrive at the conclusion that, during its movement, the stone was subjected to various influences. If the only influence had been the impulse I gave by throwing it, it would fly in a straight line forever with no change in velocity. The earth also exercises an influence on the stone. It pulls on the stone. If I had simply let go of the stone without throwing it, it would have fallen vertically to the earth. While falling, its velocity would have constantly increased. The reciprocal action of these two influences produces what I actually see.

But what if I were unable to separate these two influences and, in thought, reconstruct what I see by bringing them into a lawful relationship with one another: all there would be is what could be seen. That form of observation would be spiritually blind, merely a perception of the stone's successive positions. In fact, however, matters do *not* remain there. The whole process occurs twice: once outside where it is seen by my eyes; then my spirit lets the whole event unfold once more, in a spiritual manner. My inner sense must be directed toward the spiritual process, which is not seen by my eye; then I become aware that I awaken the spiritual aspect of that process with my own forces. One may again cite a passage from J. G. Fichte that makes this clear:

> The new sense is the sense for the spirit. It is a sense for which *only* spirit exists and nothing else; for which the other (given) existence also assumes the manner of spirit, becoming transformed into it; and for which, as a result, existence in its own right has actually disappeared.[11]
>
> This sense has been used for seeing as long as humankind has existed. Everything great and excellent in the world, and which alone enables humanity to endure, originates in the visions of this sense. But it was not true that this sense saw itself as different from and in opposition to the other, ordinary sense. Rather, the impressions of those two senses were fused together; life then split into these two halves without a unifying bond.[12]

This unifying bond is created through the fact that the inner sense recognizes the spiritual in what it awakens through its communication with the outer world. Consequently, what we take up into our spirit from the things of the outer world no longer appears as a meaningless repetition. In contrast to what external perception can impart, it emerges as something new. The simple process of throwing a stone, as well as my perception of it, are seen in a higher light once I clarify the role of my inner sense in this matter. To combine the two influences and their characteristic actions conceptually, I must already have acquired a basis of understanding when perceiving the flying stone. Thus I apply the concepts already stored within me when confronted by something in the external world. The new phenomenon integrates itself into the already present spiritual content. It reveals itself in its singularity as an expression of this content. Through the comprehension of my inner sense, I can recognize the relationship between what is acquired through this sense and the things of the external world.

Fichte was able to say, without comprehending this sense, that the world splits in half for me – things outside of me, and images of these things within me. The two halves are united when the inner sense understands *itself* and realizes what light it gives to the outer world through understanding. Fichte could also say that this inner sense sees *only* spirit. It sees how spirit brings clarity to the sensory world by integrating it into the world of spirit. The inner sense allows external, sensory existence to arise within it as a spiritual essence on a higher level. An external object is completely known when there is no part of it that has not experienced a spiritual rebirth in this way. Every outer object thus finds its place within a spiritual content, which, when grasped by the inner faculty, shares the destiny of self-knowledge. The spiritual content belonging to something enters the world of ideas completely through illumination from within, as does our own self. This explanation contains nothing that can be proven *logically*, nor is this necessary. It is nothing other than a result of inner experiences. Those who deny its claim merely reveal that they lack such inner experience. It is pointless to dispute such a matter with them, just as it would be to dispute color with a blind person.

It should not be claimed, however, that such inner experience is only possible for a gifted few. It is a general human characteristic. Anyone who does not reject it can take the path to its attainment, but such rejection is not unusual. One always has the feeling, when encountering objections in this vein, that it is not a question of not being able to acquire inner experience, but a matter of blocking one's access to it with a multiplicity of logical chimeras. It is almost like looking through a telescope, seeing a new planet, and still denying its existence because *calculations* do not indicate a planet in that particular location.

At the same time, most people definitely feel that there is more to outer nature than is to be found through the ordinary senses and analytical reason. They believe, though, that this too is to be found in the outer world, as are the objects of external perception themselves. They think it must be something that has yet to be discovered. What should be achieved through the inner sense by re-cognizing on a higher level what has been perceived and understood, they consider to be an inaccessible part of the world outside of them. They then speak of limits of knowledge that prevent us from knowing the "thing in itself." They speak of the unknown "essence" of things and are unwilling to acknowledge that this essence becomes clear when the inner sense lets its light fall upon them.

An especially revealing example of the mistake buried in this attitude was furnished in 1876 by the scientist Du Bois-Reymond in his well-known speech, "Ignorabimus."[13] According to him, we should limit ourselves to seeing manifestations of "matter" in natural processes. We cannot know anything about the nature of matter itself. Du Bois-Reymond asserts that we can never get to the point where matter "haunts" space. But the reason we cannot get to this point is that nothing at all can be found there. Whoever speaks as does Du Bois-Reymond has a feeling that any scientific understanding of nature produces results that point to something else, which this understanding cannot provide. Du Bois-Reymond does not, however, wish to take the path that leads to this "something else" – that is, to inner experience. Consequently, when confronting the question of "matter," he is baffled as though facing an impenetrable riddle. For those who take the path of inner experience, phenomena are reborn; those aspects of them that for outer experience remain unknown, become clear.

Thus, the inner life of the human being not only brings clarity to itself, but it clarifies outer reality as well. From this perspective, an infinite vista opens before human cognition. Within is the glow of a light whose luminosity is not confined to the interior. It is a sun that illuminates *all* of reality at once. Something appears within us that unites us with the world as a whole. We are no longer merely a single, accidental person, no longer this or that individual. The whole world reveals itself within us. It lays bare the nature of its coherency and shows us how we, as individuals, are connected to it. Knowledge of the world is born from self-knowledge. Our own limited individuality assumes its spiritual place in the grand, interconnected web of the world because something comes to life within us that reaches beyond our individuality and embraces everything in which our individuality participates.

Thinking that does not use logical prejudices to block its own path to inner experience will always come to recognize the essential nature acting within us. This essential nature connects us with the whole world because through it, we overcome the contrast of inner and outer in relation to ourselves. Paul Asmus, a clear-sighted philosopher, who died young, comments on this situation (*The 'I' and the Thing in Itself*):[14]

> We can become clearer about this matter through an example. Imagine a piece of sugar; it is round, sweet, impenetrable, and so on. These are qualities we all understand. There is only one thing that seems to be completely different and beyond our understanding – something so different from us that we cannot penetrate it without losing ourselves; our thought timidly recoils from the mere surface of it. This one thing, which is still unknown to us, is the carrier of all these qualities; it is the essence that constitutes the innermost self of that object. Thus, Hegel correctly says that the whole content of our idea is related to this unfathomable subject only coincidentally and that we qualify this essence without really getting to the bottom of it. Since we do not know this essence itself, such qualifications ultimately have no real objective value, being only subjective.
>
> With a thinking that is able to comprehend, however, we do not encounter an unknowable subject whose qualifications are only accidental; *rather, the objective subject falls within the concept.* If I comprehend something, it is completely present in my concept. I am at home in the innermost sanctuary of its nature – not because it lacks its own essence, but because it compels me *through the necessity, hovering above us both*, of the concept (which appears subjectively in me and objectively in it) to *re*-think its concept. As Hegel says, through this *re*-thinking, it is

> revealed to us that just as this is our subjective activity, *it is at the same time the true nature of the object.*

Only those who can illuminate the processes of thinking with the light of inner experience can speak in this way.

In my *Philosophy of Spiritual Activity*, I have also pointed, from another perspective, to the primordial fact of the inner life:[15]

> It is therefore beyond any doubt that in thinking we grasp world-happening by a corner where we must be present if something is to come about. And that is, after all, exactly the point. That is exactly the reason why things confront me as such a riddle: because I am so uninvolved in their coming about. I simply find them before me; with thinking, however, I know how it is done. Thus there is no starting point for looking at all world-happening more primal than thinking.

For those who view inner experience in this way, the meaning of human cognition within the context of the whole is clear. It is not an empty addition to what occurs in the universe. This would be the case if it only reiterated external existence in the form of ideas. But in *cognition*, something takes place that does not occur anywhere in the outer world: universal existence is confronted with its own spiritual nature. The universal process would always remain only half-complete if that confrontation did not take place. With it, our inner experience is integrated into the objective, universal process; without it, the universal process would be incomplete.

It is evident that only a life governed by the inner sense, our highest spiritual life in the truest sense, lifts us above ourselves. For only in this life is the nature of things revealed in the encounter with itself. It is different for the lower faculties of perception. The eye, for example, that mediates the visual perception of an object, is the location of a process that, for the inner life, is identical to any other outer process. Like other things, my organs are parts of the spatial world, and their perceptions are temporal processes like others. Their essential nature also becomes apparent only when immersed in inner experience.

Consequently, I live a double life: the life of a thing among things that exists within its corporeality, and through its organs perceives what exists outside that corporeality; and a higher life above this one that knows no inside and outside and extends over both the external world and itself. I must therefore say that at one moment I am an individual, limited 'I,' and at another, I am a universal 'I.'

This, too, Paul Asmus has put into appropriate words (*The Indo-Germanic Religion in Its Main Points of Development*):[16]

> When we immerse ourselves in something else, we call it "thinking." In thinking, the 'I' has fulfilled its concept; it has surrendered its separate existence. Therefore, in thinking, we find ourselves in a realm that is the same for everyone,

> because the principle of isolation (which is the nature of the relationship between the 'I' and what is different from it) has disappeared into the activity of the 'I' suspending its separateness. There is only *'I'-being common to all.*

This is exactly what Spinoza has in mind when he states that the highest activity of cognition proceeds "from an adequate idea of certain attributes of God to an adequate knowledge of the essence of things."[17] This progression is simply the illumination of things by the light of inner experience. Spinoza describes the life of this inner experience in glorious colors:

> The highest virtue of the soul is to know God, or to understand things by the third – highest – kind of knowledge. This virtue is ever greater, the more the soul knows things by this kind of knowledge: he who grasps things through this kind of knowledge reaches the summit of human perfection and is consequently filled with the greatest joy, and indeed accompanied by the ideas of his self and of virtue. Thus, from this kind of knowledge arises the highest possible calmness of soul.[18]

Whoever comprehends things in this way transforms himself from within, because at such moments his separate 'I' is absorbed by the All-'I.' All beings do not appear as having a significance subordinate to a separate, limited individual; they appear as themselves. At this level there is no difference between Plato and me; what separates us belongs to a lower level of cognition.

We are separated only as individuals; the universal nature acting in us is one and the same. One cannot dispute this fact with a person who has not experienced it. Such a person will always insist that Plato and I are two. This duality – that all multiplicity is reborn as unity in the development of the highest level of knowing – cannot be proven; it must be *experienced.* Paradoxical as it may sound, it is true. The idea that Plato represented to himself and the same idea that I represent to myself are not two ideas. They are one and the same idea. These ideas do not exist separately – one in Plato's head and the other in mine. Instead, in a higher sense, Plato's head and mine interpenetrate; all heads that grasp the same *single* idea interpenetrate. This unique idea exists only once. It is there, and the heads all transport themselves to one and the same place in order to have this idea within them.

The transformation that takes place in the whole character of the human being when one adopts this view is shown beautifully in the Bhagavad Gita, the ancient Sanskrit epic. Wilhelm von Humboldt said that he thanked his destiny for allowing him to live long enough to become acquainted with this work.[19] In this poem, the Inner Light speaks thus:

> An eternal ray of mine, which has acquired a particular existence in the world of personal life, draws to itself the five senses and the individual soul, which belong to nature. When the outshining spirit is embodied in space and

> time, or when it is disembodied, it grasps the things and takes them with it, as the breath of wind grasps the fragrances of flowers and carries them forth. The Inner Light presides over ear, feeling, taste, and smell, as well as over the soul; it creates the bond between itself and the things of the senses. The foolish do not know when the Inner Light begins to shine or when it extinguishes, nor when it weds itself to the things. Only those who partake in the Inner Light can know of such matters.[20]

So strongly does the Bhagavad Gita point to the transformation of the human being that it says of the "sage" that he can no longer err or sin. If he seems to err or sin, then he must be illuminating his thoughts or actions with a light through which what seems like sin or error to ordinary consciousness no longer appears as such. "He who has elevated himself, and whose cognition is of the purest nature, does not kill and does not defile himself, even if he should slay another."[21] This indicates the same basic disposition of soul, springing from the highest cognition, about which Spinoza, after describing it in his *Ethics*, pours forth these captivating words:

> I have thus completed all I wished to set forth concerning the soul's power over the emotions and the soul's freedom. Whence it appears, how potent are the wise, and how much they surpass the ignorant, who are driven only by lusts. For the ignorant are not only distracted in various ways by external causes without ever

> gaining true calmness of soul, but moreover live, as it were, unaware of themselves, God, and things; and as soon as they cease to suffer, they cease also to be. Whereas the wise, insofar as they are to be regarded as such, are scarcely disturbed at all in spirit – and being conscious of themselves, God, and things, through a certain eternal necessity, never cease to be, but always possess true calmness of soul. If the way I have pointed out as leading to this result seems exceedingly hard, nevertheless it may indeed be discovered. It must be hard since it is so seldom found. If salvation were readily available and could be found without great labor, how could it possibly be neglected by almost everyone? All that is sublime, however, is as difficult as it is rare.[22]

Goethe outlined, in a monumental way, the perspective of the highest knowledge: "If I know my relationship to myself and to the outer world, then I call it *truth*. And in this way, each person can have his own truth, and it is after all always the same one."[23] Everyone has his own truth because each person is an individual, distinct being alongside and together with others. Those other beings act upon the individual through the organs of perception. From the particular point of view that the individual adopts, and depending on the nature of his ability to perceive, he develops his own truth in association with the things he meets. He acquires his own relationship to things. Then, when he attains self-knowledge, he learns to know his relationship to himself, and the particular truth dissolves into the general truth; this general truth is the same for everyone.

Those with deeper understanding see in the raising up of the individual, in the transformation of the separate 'I' becoming All-'I,' the mystery that reveals itself within the human being, the primordial mystery of life. Goethe also found an apt expression for this: "And so long you do not have this: Die and so become! – you are but a dreary guest upon a gloomy earth."[24]

What takes place in the human inner life is not a conceptual reiteration but an actual part of the universal process. The world would not be what it is if what also belongs to it did not take place within the human soul. And if one names the highest that a human being can attain "divine," then one must also say that the divine is not something external to be recapitulated as an *image* in the human spirit. Rather, one must say that the divine is *awakened* within the human being. Angelus Silesius found the right words for this: "I know that *without me* God cannot live for a moment; if I come to nothing, He must give up the ghost." He goes on to say, "God cannot make a single worm without me; it would immediately fall apart if I did not preserve it with Him."[25] Such an assertion can come only from one who has realized that there is something in the human being without which no external being could exist. If all that belongs to the "worm" could exist without the human being, then it could not be said that the worm would "fall apart" without the human being there to preserve it.

The innermost core of the world comes to life as spiritual substance. For the human being, the experience of self-knowledge means becoming actively mobile within the germinal heart of the universe. Those who are imbued with self-knowledge also naturally conduct their own actions in the light of self-knowledge. Typically, human action is determined by *motives*. The poet and philosopher Robert Hamerling has rightly said (in *The Atomistic Nature of the Will*):[26]

> It is true that the human being can do what he wills, but he cannot will what he wills because his will is determined by *motives*! He cannot will what he wills? Let us look more closely at these words. Does the meaning contained therein stand to reason? Would free will thus consist in the ability to will something without motive or reason? But what does it mean to will if not to *have a reason* for one's preference to do or aspire to one thing rather than another? To will without cause or motive would mean to will *without willing it*. Motive as a concept is inseparably related to that of willing. Without a definite motive, the will is an empty *capacity*; only motive makes it active and real. It is indeed correct to say that the human will is not free insofar as its direction is always determined by the strongest motive.

For every action that does not take place in the light of self-knowledge, the motive, the cause of the action, must be felt as a compulsion. It is a different matter when the cause falls within the bounds of self-knowledge. In this case, the cause becomes part of the self. The will is no longer determined; it determines itself. The lawfulness, the motives of the will no longer rule *over* the one who would act, but rather are identical with the will to act. To illuminate one's actions with the light of self-observation means to overcome all compulsion. In this way, the will places itself within the realm of *freedom*.

Not all human actions are free. Only action that has been warmed through and through by self-observation is free. Because self-observation lifts the individual 'I' to the All-'I,' free action flows forth from the All-'I.' The old dispute as to whether the human will is free or subordinated to general, unalterable necessity is an incorrectly posed question. Actions performed by a person as an individual are not free; actions performed by a person after spiritual rebirth are free. The human being is not, in some all-encompassing sense, *either* free *or* not free. He is *just as much one as the other*. He is unfree before his rebirth, and he can *become* free through this rebirth. The higher evolution of the individual human being rests on the *transformation* of unfree willing into willing with the character of freedom. The person who has permeated the lawfulness of his actions in such a way as to make it his own has overcome the compulsion of that lawfulness and, with this, his own lack of freedom. Freedom is not a *given* in human existence; rather, it is a *goal.*

In free action, the human being resolves a contradiction between the world and himself. His own actions become acts of universal existence. He experiences himself in complete harmony with this universal existence. He feels every dissonance between himself and another as the result of a not yet fully awakened self. But it is the destiny of the self that only in its separation from the universal can it find the connection to this universal. The human being would not be human if he were not set apart from everything else as an individual 'I.' But he would also not in the highest sense be human if he did not expand himself from individual 'I' to All-'I.' It belongs to the essence of human nature that it should overcome a contradiction originally laid within it.

A person for whom spirit means only intellectual logic may feel his blood run cold at the thought that things are to experience their rebirth in the spirit. He will compare a fresh, living flower outside, in all the richness of its colors, to a cold, pale, diagrammatic *thought* of the flower. He becomes especially uncomfortable at the idea that people who find the motives for their actions in the seclusion of the conscious self are freer than those who are spontaneous and naïve and who act impulsively out of the fullness of their nature. To anyone who can only see the one-sided, logical aspect, the person who immerses himself in his inner life will appear to be a walking conceptual schema, like a ghost in contrast to a person who remains planted firmly in his natural individuality.

Similar arguments against the rebirth of the world of objects in the spirit are often brought forth eloquently by those with healthy senses and lively drives and passions but who are ill-equipped to observe objects of purely spiritual substance. When they encounter something spiritual, they lack the corresponding intuitions; all that is there for them are hollow concepts or even empty words. Therefore, when the matter of spiritual significance arises, they remain "dry," "abstract intellectuals." But for those who are able to observe in the purely spiritual realm as well as in the sensory realm, life naturally does not become poorer if it is enriched with spirit. If I look at a flower, why should its rich colors lose any freshness if it is not only my eye that sees the colors but *also* my inner sense that sees the spiritual nature of that flower? Why should the life of my personality become poorer because I do not follow my passions and impulses in spiritual blindness, but instead illuminate them with the light of a higher cognition? The life reflected in spirit is not poorer but fuller and richer.[a]

[a] See addendum I, p. 171.

.I.

MEISTER ECKHART

The conceptual world of Meister Eckhart is fully aglow with the sense that things are reborn as higher realities in human consciousness. He belonged to the Order of the Dominicans, as did the greatest Christian theologian of the Middle Ages, Thomas Aquinas, who lived from 1225 to 1274. Eckhart had a deep admiration for Aquinas. This is fully understandable when one examines the manner of his thinking in its entirety. He considered himself to be in harmony with the teachings of the Christian Church to the same degree that he assumed Aquinas to be. Eckhart did not want to take anything away from the meaning of Christianity, nor did he want to add anything to it. He wanted to produce this content anew in *his* way. A person such as he did not have the spiritual need to replace old truths with some variety of new ones. He had grown to be one with what he had learned. But he wanted to give a new form, a new life, to it. Without a doubt, he wanted to remain an orthodox Christian. The Christian truths were *his* truths. Only he wanted to look at them in a different way than had Thomas Aquinas, for instance.

Aquinas assumed two sources of knowledge: *revelation* for faith and *reason* for inquiry. Reason understands the laws of things; that is, the spiritual element in nature. It can also raise itself above nature and, in spirit, grasp from one side the divine essence underlying all nature. But in this way, it does not achieve immersion in the *full* essence of God. A higher form of truth must come to meet it. This truth is given in the scriptures. Scriptures *reveal* what a human being cannot attain on his own. A person must accept the truth of the scriptures; reason can defend it and try to understand it as well as possible, but reason can never produce this truth out of the human spirit. It is not what the spirit *sees* that is the *highest* truth, but a certain cognitive content that has come to the spirit *from outside.* Saint Augustine declares that he is incapable of finding within himself the source of what he *should believe.* He says, "I would not believe the Gospel if the authority of the Catholic Church did not move me to do so."[27] This is stated in the sense of the Evangelist, who refers us to the external testimony: "That which was from the beginning, which we have heard, which we have seen with our eyes, which we have looked upon, and our hands have handled, of the Word of Life. . . . That which we have seen and heard declare we unto you, that ye also may have fellowship with us."[28]

Meister Eckhart wishes to impress Christ's words upon us: "It is expedient for you that I go away: for if I go not away, the Comforter will not come unto you; but if I depart, I will send him unto you."[29] And he explains these words by saying, "It is as though He were to say: 'You have taken too much joy in my *present image*; therefore the perfect joy of the Holy Spirit cannot be in you.'"[30] Eckhart thinks that he is speaking of no God other than the one spoken of by Augustine, the Evangelist, and Aquinas; and yet, their testimony of God is not his testimony:

> Some people want to look upon God with their eyes, as they look upon a cow, and want to love God as they love a cow. They love God for the sake of external riches and internal solace, but these people do not love God properly.[31]
>
> The foolish believe they should conceive of God as though He stood there, and they here. But this is not how it is. God and I are one in the act of knowing.[32]

Such declarations by Eckhart are based on an experience of the inner sense. This experience illuminates matters with a higher light. Consequently, he does not think that he needs an external light to attain the highest insights:

> A master speaks: God has become flesh; through this, all are raised and exalted. Let us rejoice that Christ our brother has ascended by His own strength above all the angelic choirs and sits at the right hand of the Father. This master has spoken well, but in truth, I do not set great store by it. What good would it do me if I had a rich brother while I remained poor? What good would it do me to have a wise brother if I were a fool?[33]
>
> The Heavenly Father brings forth His only begotten Son in Himself and *in me.* Why in

> Himself and in me? I am united with Him, and He cannot shut me out. In the same act, the Holy Spirit receives its being and arises through me as it does through God. Why? I am in God, and if the Holy Spirit does not take its being from me, neither does it take it from God. I am in no way excluded.[34]

When Eckhart reminds us of the words of Paul, "But put ye on the Lord Jesus Christ,"[35] he wishes to give these words this meaning: Turn your gaze inward; immerse yourselves in self-contemplation, and from the depths of your being God will shine upon you; He will illuminate everything for you. You will have found Him within yourselves; you will have become united with God's essence. "God has become human so that I might become God."[36] In his treatise *On Solitude*, Eckhart expresses himself on the relationship of external to internal perception:

> Here you must know that the masters say that in each human being there are two kinds of people. The first is called the outer human being, that is, sensuality; the human being is served by five senses, and yet acts through the force of the soul. The other person is called the inner human being, that is, the human inner life. Now you must realize that those who love God do not use the forces of the soul in the outer human being any more than is needed by the five senses. The inner human being does not turn to the five senses except as a director and guide. The inner human being watches over

> them so that, in their work, they do not pander to animal nature.[37]

Whoever speaks in this manner about the inner human being can no longer focus on a sense-perceptible *essence* of something existing *outside himself*. For it is clear to him that this *essence* is not to be encountered in any aspect of the sense-perceptible outer world. One could object: What do things of the outside world have to do with what you add to them from your spirit? Trust your senses. Only they give you knowledge of the outside world. Do not falsify with spiritual adornment what your senses give you without decoration, in purity, as a picture of the outer world. Your eye tells you the nature of a color; nothing of what your spirit apprehends about color is in the color. From Meister Eckhart's perspective, one would have to reply that the senses are physical devices. Accordingly, what they communicate about phenomena relates only to the physical characteristics of things. These physical aspects make themselves known to me by stimulating a physical process within me.

Color as a physical process of the outer world produces a corresponding physical process in my eye and in my brain. Through it, I perceive the color. But in this way, I can perceive in the color only what is physical, the sensory aspects. Sensory perception excludes all those features that are not sensory. It divests phenomena of all that is not sensory in them. If I then proceed to the spiritual, the ideal meaning, then I reestablish only those aspects of phenomena that sensory perception has erased. Hence, sensory perception does not show me the deepest nature of things; rather, it separates me from this nature. Spiritual comprehension, comprehension through the idea, again connects me with this nature. It shows me that, within themselves, objects of the natural world are of exactly the same spiritual nature as I am.

The boundary between the external world and myself is abolished by spiritual comprehension of the world. I am separated from the external world insofar as I am a sense-perceptible object within the context of the sensory world. My eye and the color are two different entities. My brain and the plant are two. But the meaning of the plant and of the color, together with the ideal meaning of my brain and of my eye, belong to a unified ideal entity.

This view must not be confused with the widespread anthropomorphizing worldview which believes that external phenomena can be comprehended by ascribing to them qualities of a psychic nature – qualities that are supposed to be similar to the qualities of the human soul. This view states that when we encounter another person, we perceive only sense-perceptible characteristics. I cannot see what lives within my fellow human beings. From what I see and hear, I infer their inner life, or soul. Consequently, the soul is something I can never perceive directly.

I perceive a soul only within myself. No other person sees my thoughts, my imagining, and my feelings. And just as *I* have such an inner life alongside the life that can be perceived externally, so must all other beings have one too. This is the conclusion of someone who adopts an anthropomorphic worldview. In the same way, the part of a plant that I perceive externally must be only the outer aspect of an interior, of a soul, which I must add, in my thoughts, to what I perceive. Since only a single inner world exists for me – my own – I can only imagine that the inner world of others is similar to mine. In this way, one reaches a sort of universal ensoulment of all nature (*panpsychism*).

This view rests upon a misunderstanding of what the developed inner sense really offers. The spiritual nature of an external object, which appears to me within myself, is not added in thought to the external perception any more than is the spirit of another human being. I perceive this spiritual content through the inner sense, just as I perceive the physical content through the external senses. And what I call my inner life, in the sense indicated above, is by no means my spirit in the higher sense. This inner life is the result of purely sensory processes; it belongs to me only as a totally individual personality, which is nothing but the result of its physical organization. When I transfer this interior life to external phenomena, I am actually indulging in idle fancy. My personal inner life – my thoughts, memories, and feelings – is part of me because I am a creature of nature with a particular organization, with a certain sensory apparatus, with an individual nervous system. I cannot transfer my *human* soul to phenomena. I could do this only if somewhere I found a similarly organized nervous system. But my individual soul is not the highest spiritual part of me. The highest spiritual part must first be awakened in me by the inner sense. What is thus awakened in me is one and the same with the spirit in all things. The plant appears before this spiritual part directly in its own spirituality. I need not endow it with a spirituality similar to my own. In terms of *this* worldview, all talk about the unknown "thing in itself" becomes devoid of meaning. It is precisely the so-called "thing in itself" that reveals itself to the inner sense.

All discussion about the unknown "thing in itself" stems from the fact that those who speak about it are incapable of recognizing within the spiritual content of their own inner lives the spiritual essence of the "things in themselves." They think that they recognize only insubstantial shadows and phantoms within themselves – the "mere concepts and ideas" of things. Nevertheless, since they have an *intimation* of the "thing in itself," they think that it conceals itself and limits the human capacity to know. One cannot prove to those who labor under this belief that they must find this "thing in itself" within themselves since they would never acknowledge it if one showed it to them. But it is precisely this *acknowledgment* that matters. Everything Meister Eckhart says is permeated by this acknowledgment:

> Consider an analogy for this. A door opens and closes on a hinge. If I compare the outer boards of the door to the external human being, then I shall compare the hinge to the inner human being. Now when the door opens and closes, the outer boards move back and forth, while the hinge remains constantly immobile and in no way is changed. And here it is the same.[38]

As an individual being of the sense world, I can investigate things in all directions – the door opens and closes. If I do not let the perceptions of the senses arise within me spiritually, I shall know nothing of their essence – the hinge does not move. In Eckhart's view, the illumination mediated by the inner sense is God's entry to the soul. He calls the light of knowledge that is lit by this entry the "spark of the soul."[39] The place within us where this spark is lighted is "so pure, and so elevated, and so noble in itself that no creature can be in it; only God alone dwells there in His pure divine nature."[40] Whoever has let this "spark" light up within no longer sees *merely* as a human being sees – with the external senses and with the logical intellect, which orders and classifies the impressions of the senses – but instead sees how things are in and of themselves.

The external senses and the ordering intellect

separate the individual human being from other things; they make him into an independent being in space and in time that also perceives other things in space and in time. The human being illuminated by the spark ceases to be an individual being. He eradicates his separateness. Everything that brings into effect a difference between him and the things around him ceases to exist. That it is *he*, as an individual entity, that perceives – this no longer even comes into consideration. The things, and thus also God, see themselves in the individual. "This spark is God, in such a way that it is united and carries within itself the image of all creatures, image without image, and image beyond image."[41] Eckhart speaks superbly of the extinguishing of the individual being:

> It must, therefore, be understood that to know God and to be known by God are the same. We know God and we see that He makes us seeing and knowing. And as the air that is illuminated is nothing other than what illuminates it, for it shines by virtue of the fact that it is illuminated – in the same way, we know that we are known and that He causes us to know Him.[42]

It is upon this foundation that Meister Eckhart builds his relationship with God. It is a purely spiritual relationship, and it cannot be formed in an image borrowed from the individual life of the human being. God cannot love His creation as one individual loves another; God cannot have created the world as a master builder constructs a house. All such thoughts disappear in the face of the inner vision. It belongs to the *being* of God that He loves the world. The image of a god who could love and also not love is formed in the image of the individual human being:

> I say in good truth and in eternal truth and in everlasting truth that into every human being who has gone within, God must pour Himself out to the limits of His ability. He must pour Himself out utterly and completely, so that He retains nothing in His life and in His being, in His nature and in His divinity. Everything must He pour out in a fruit-bearing manner.[43]

And inner illumination is something that the soul *must* find when it turns its gaze toward the depths of its being. It becomes evident that the way God speaks to humankind cannot be thought of in the image of the *revelation* of one human being to another. For *this* way of communicating can also be forgone. A person can close himself off to another. God *must* communicate Himself, in conformity with His nature:

> It is a secure truth that God has the need to seek us as if all His divinity depended upon it. God can no more do without us than we can do without Him. Although we may turn away from God, God can never turn away from us.[44]

Consequently, the relationship of the human being to God cannot be understood as containing anything figurative borrowed from what is *individually* human. Eckhart realizes that part of the fulfillment of the primal being of the world is that it should find itself in the human soul. This primal being would be imperfect, even unfinished, if it lacked that component of its nature that appears in the human soul. What takes place in the human being belongs to the primal being; and if it were not to take place, then the primal being would be only a fraction of itself. In this way, the human being can sense that he is a *necessary* part of the being of the world. Eckhart expresses this by describing his feelings toward God as follows:

> I do not thank God for loving me, for He cannot keep from doing so; whether He wants to or not, His nature compels Him to it. . . . Therefore I shall not plead with God to give me something; I also will not praise Him for what He has given me.[45]

This relationship of the human soul to the primal being must not be understood to mean that the soul, in its individual character, is explained by the relationship. The soul, entangled as it is in the world of the senses and thus in what is finite, does *not* already bear within itself the substance of this primal being. It must first develop it within. It must obliterate itself as an individual being. Meister Eckhart has aptly characterized this obliteration as an "*un-becoming.*" "When I come into the ground of Divinity, no one asks me whence I come and where I have been, and no one misses me, for here there is an *un-becoming.*"[46]

This relationship is also clearly described in the following passage:

> I take a basin of water, place a mirror in it, and put it under the wheel of the sun. The sun casts its luminous radiance on the mirror, and yet it is not diminished. The reflection of the mirror in the sun is sun in the sun, and yet the mirror is what it is. Thus it is with God. God is in the soul with His nature and in His being and His divinity, and yet He is not the soul. The reflection of the soul in God is God in God, and yet the soul is what it is.

The soul that gives itself over to inner illumination recognizes in itself not only what it was *before* illumination but also what it has become only *through* this illumination:

> We are to be united with God essentially. We are to be united with God as one. We are to be united with God completely. How are we to be united with God essentially? This is to be accomplished by seeing and not by being. His being cannot become our being, but it is to be our life.[47]

It is not an already existing life – "being" – that is to be understood in a logical sense; rather, higher understanding – "seeing" – is itself to become life. The spiritual, the ideal may be experienced by the seeing human being in the same way as the individual human nature experiences ordinary, everyday life.

From such points of departure, Meister Eckhart also finds his way to a pure *concept of freedom*. In ordinary life, the soul is not free. It is entangled in the realm of lower causes. It accomplishes what it is compelled to do by these lower causes. "Seeing" raises it out of the realm of these causes. It no longer acts as an individual soul. In it is laid open the primal essence, which cannot be caused by anything except itself:

> God does not compel the will; rather, He sets it at liberty, so that it wills nothing but what God Himself wills. Spirit can will nothing but what God wills. This is not a lack of freedom; it is the spirit's true freedom. For freedom is this: that we are not bound, that we are free and pure and unadulterated, as we were in our first origin and when we were wed in the Holy Spirit.[48]

It may be said of the enlightened human being that he is the entity that determines good and evil from out of himself. He cannot do otherwise than accomplish the good. For he does not serve the good; rather, the good lives itself out through him. "The righteous person serves neither God nor the created beings, because he is free, and the closer he is to righteousness, the more he is freedom itself."[49] What, then, must evil be for Meister Eckhart? It can only be acting under the influence of the lower way of seeing, the action of a soul that has not passed through the state of *un-becoming*. Such a soul is selfish in the sense that it wills only *itself*. Only outwardly could it bring its willing into harmony with moral ideals. The seeing soul cannot be selfish in this sense. Even should it will *itself*, it would still will the mastery of the ideal, for it has made itself into this ideal. It can no longer will the goals of the lower nature, for it no longer has anything in common with this lower nature. It is no matter of compulsion, no matter of deprivation, for the seeing soul to act in the sense of moral ideals:

> For the person who stands in God's will and in God's love, it is a *joy* to do all the good things God wills and to leave undone all the evil things that are against God. And it is impossible for such a person to leave a thing undone that God wants to have accomplished. As it would be impossible for one to walk whose legs are bound, so it would be impossible for one to do ill who is in God's will.[50]

Furthermore, Eckhart emphatically protests an interpretation that would see in his view a license for one to do whatever one wants. We only recognize the seeing human being in the fact that a person no longer wants anything as an individual:

> There are those who say, "If I have God and God's freedom, then I can do whatever I want." They understand these words amiss. As long as you can do anything that is against God and His commandments, you do not have God's love; you can only deceive the world into the belief that you have it.[51]

Eckhart is convinced that the soul that plumbs its own depths encounters there a perfect morality. There all logical understanding and all action in the ordinary sense have an end, and an entirely new order of human life begins:

> For everything the understanding can grasp, and everything desire demands, is not God. Where the understanding and desire end, there it is dark, and there God shines. There that power unfolds in the soul which is wider than the wide heavens.[52]
>
> The blessedness of the righteous and God's blessedness is one and the same blessedness; for the righteous one is blessed because God is blessed.[53]

.II.
FRIENDSHIP WITH GOD

Those movements of the soul that are aroused in profound natures by a spiritual path such as that of Meister Eckhart appear most impressively in the lives and works of Johannes Tauler (1300–1361), Heinrich Suso (1295–1366), and Jan van Ruysbroeck (1293–1381). If Eckhart seems to be a man who, in the blissful experience of spiritual rebirth, speaks of the qualities and nature of knowledge as of a picture he has succeeded in painting, then the others appear as wanderers to whom this rebirth has shown a new path. They wish to travel this path, although the end of it seems to them to have been removed to an infinite distance. Eckhart describes the splendors of his picture; they characterize the difficulties of the new path.

One must be very clear about the relationship of the human being to higher knowledge before attempting to grasp the difference between individuals such as Eckhart and Tauler. The human being is entangled in the sensory world and the natural lawfulness that governs it; he himself is a product of this world. He lives because its forces and substances are active in him, and he perceives and judges the world of the senses according to the laws that have constructed it and himself. When he directs his gaze to an object, not only does the object appear as a sum of interacting forces ruled by the laws of nature, but the eye itself is also a body constructed according to such laws and forces.

The act of seeing takes place in harmony with these laws and forces. If we were to reach the utmost limits of natural science, then we could indeed pursue the play of natural forces in accordance with natural laws into the highest regions of thinking. But in doing so, we rise *above* this play of natural forces. Have we not found a position above mere conformity to natural laws when we *survey* how we ourselves are integrated into nature? We *see* with our eyes in conformity with the laws of nature, but we also *understand* the laws that govern the activity of seeing. We can stand on a higher elevation and simultaneously survey the external world and ourselves in interplay.

Is there not something active within us that is higher than the organic, sensory personality, which acts according to natural laws and with the forces of nature? Is there in such activity still a partition between our inner world and the external world? What here judges, what works through to clarity, is no longer our individual personality; rather, it is the universal world-essence, which has torn down the barrier between inner world and outer world and which now embraces both.

Just as it is true that I retain outwardly my individual separateness when I have torn down the barrier, so is it also true that, *in essence*, I am no longer this individual. The feeling now lives in me that in my soul the universal being speaks, the being that embraces the whole world and me. Such feelings live in Tauler when he says:

> The human being is truly, as it were, three people: an animal being, as he is according to the senses; a being of reason; and finally, the highest, divinely-formed godlike being.[54]
>
> One is the external, animal-like, sensory human being; the other is the internal, rational human being, with powers of reason; and the third human being is the inner spirit [*Gemüt*], the absolute highest part of the soul.[55] (See W. Preger, *History of German Mysticism.*)[56]

Eckhart has expressed, in the following words, how this third human being is superior to the first and second: "The eye through which I see God is the same eye through which God sees me. My eye and God's eye are one eye and one seeing and one knowing and one feeling."[57] But alongside this sentiment, another one lives in Tauler. He struggles through to a real concept of spirit, and he does not continually intermingle the sensory with the spiritual world, as do false materialists and false idealists. If Tauler, with his way of thinking, had become a scientist, he would have had to insist that everything natural, including the *whole* human being – the first and the second being – could be explained in accordance with nature. He would never have transferred "purely" spiritual forces into nature. He would not have spoken of an anthropomorphic "functionalism" in nature. He knew that where we perceive with the senses, no "Creation-thoughts" [*Schöpfungsgedanken*] are to be found. Instead, he was unwaveringly conscious of the fact that the human being is a merely natural being. Since he felt himself to be a caretaker of the moral life – and not a scientist – he saw the contrast that separates this natural aspect of the human being from the "seeing" of God, which arises in a natural way within the natural world, but as something spiritual.

It was in this contrast that the meaning of life appeared before his eyes. The human being is an individual being, a creature of nature. No science can reveal anything more to a human being about this life than that he is such a creature. As a being of nature, he cannot transcend natural existence. He must remain within it. And yet, his inner life leads him beyond it. He must have trust in something that no science of external nature can give him or show him. If he calls nature "existence," he must be able to advance to the view that acknowledges nonexistence as the higher order. Tauler does not seek a god who exists in the sense of a natural force; he does not seek a god who has created the world in the way humans create. The awareness lived in him that even the concept of Creation held by the teachers of the Church is only an idealized human form of creating. It is clear to him that God is not found in the same manner that science finds natural processes and natural laws. Tauler knows that we cannot simply add God to nature in our thoughts. He knows that one who conceives of God in this manner has no more content in that thought than one who has apprehended nature in thought. Consequently, Tauler does not want to think God; he wants to think divinely. Knowledge of nature is not *enriched* through divine knowledge; it is *transformed*. A person who knows divinely does not know something *different* from the one who knows nature; such a person *knows differently*. One who knows *as God* cannot add a single letter to the knowledge of nature, but through this knowledge of nature a new light shines.

The basic sensations that dominate the soul of a person who looks at the world from such points of view will depend on how this individual regards the experience of the soul brought about by spiritual rebirth. Within this experience, the human being is wholly a being of nature when he sees himself interacting with the rest of nature. And he is wholly a spiritual being when he considers the condition that results from his transformation. It may be said with equal justification, therefore, that the greatest depths of the soul are still natural, yet also already divine. In conformity with his way of thinking, Tauler emphasized the former. No matter how deeply we penetrate our souls, he told himself, we always remain individual human beings. Nevertheless, universal being shines forth in the depths of the individual soul.

Tauler was dominated by the feeling: You

cannot detach yourself from your individuality; you cannot cleanse yourself of it. Accordingly, the universal essence cannot appear in its purity within you; it can only shine into the depths of your soul. Thus, only a reflection, an *image* of the universal essence appears. You can transform your individual personality so that it gives back the image of the universal essence; the essence itself does not shine within you. From such notions, Tauler came to the idea of a Divinity that never entirely merges with the human world, never flows into it. It was important to him that he not be confused with those who declare the interior of the human being to be something divine in itself. He says that the union with God

> is thought by ignorant human beings to occur in the flesh, and they say that they should be transformed into divine nature. This is a false and evil heresy. Even in the highest and most intimate union with God, the divine nature and God's essence are high, indeed higher than all height. This leads into a divine abyss, and no creature will ever partake of it.[58]

Deservedly, in the tenor of his time and of his vocation as a priest, Tauler wants to be called a believing Catholic. He has no intention of confronting Christianity with another point of view. He simply wants to deepen and spiritualize Christianity through his views. He speaks as a pious priest of the contents of scripture. Nevertheless, in his world of ideas the scriptures become a means of expression for the innermost experiences of his soul:

> God accomplishes all His works in the soul and gives them to the soul, and the Father brings forth His only begotten Son in the soul as truly as He brings Him forth in eternity, neither less nor more. What is brought forth when one says, "God brings forth in the soul"? Is it a likeness of God, or is it an image of God, or is it something else of God? No, it is neither image nor likeness of God but the same God and the same Son whom the Father brings forth in eternity, and nothing other than this. For the loving, divine Word, which is the other person in the Trinity – this is what the Father brings forth in the soul . . . and it is from this that the soul derives such a great and special worthiness.[59] (See Preger, *History of German Mysticism*.)[60]

Tauler viewed the narratives of the scriptures as the garment in which he would clothe the events of the inner life:

> Herod, who drove away the Child and wanted to kill him, is an image of the world, which still wants to kill this Child in the devout person. One should and must flee this world if one wants to keep the Child alive within, because the Child is the enlightened, faithful soul of every human being.[61]

Because Tauler directs his attention to the natural human being, he is less concerned with describing what happens when the higher human being enters into the natural human being than with finding the paths that the lower forces of the personality must take if they are to be converted into the higher life. As a caretaker of the moral life, he wants to show the human being the ways to universal being. He has absolute faith and confidence that the universal being will begin to shine forth in the human being if the human being arranges his life so as to make a place for the Divine. But this universal being can never begin to shine forth if the human being shuts himself off in his merely natural, separate personality. Isolated within himself, in the language of Tauler, the human being is just a part of the world, an individual creature. The more the human being encloses himself within his existence as part of the world, the less can universal being find a place within him:

> If one is to become truly one with God, all the forces of the internal person must die and become silent. The will must be turned away from even the good and from all willing and must become "without will."[62]
>
> The person should escape all the senses, turn all his faculties inward, and come into a forgetting of all things and of his self.[63]
>
> For the true and eternal Word of God is only spoken in the desert once a person has left behind his self and all things, and stands in complete solitude, desolate and lonely.[64]

When Tauler had reached his highest point, the following question became his central concern:

How can people destroy and overcome their individual inner existence, so that they can take part in universal life? For those who are in this situation, their feelings toward universal being become concentrated in only one thing – reverence for it, as for the inexhaustible and infinite. They say to themselves, "No matter what level one has attained, there are still higher prospects, still more sublime possibilities." They are clear about the direction they must take; it is equally clear that one can never speak of a goal.

A new goal is only the beginning of a new path. With a new goal, a person has reached a certain *degree of development*; development itself extends into the immeasurable. At the present level, one can never know what will be achieved at a more distant level. We cannot *know* the final goal; we can only *trust* the path, the process of development. It is possible to arrive at a knowledge of everything the human being has achieved. It consists in penetrating an already existing object with faculties of the spirit. For the higher inner life, knowledge *of this nature* does not exist. Here the faculties of the spirit must first translate the object itself into existence; they must first *create* an existence for it that is like natural existence. Natural science examines the evolution of living beings from the simplest creature to the most perfect, the human being. *This* evolutionary process lies completed before us. We understand it by penetrating it with our mental faculties. Once evolution arrives at the human being, we *find* no continuation already in existence. We bring about the continuation ourselves. We now *live* what we only *knew* at earlier levels. We *recreate* objectively, according to our spiritual natures, what we only *reproduced* at preceding stages.

The truth does not coincide only with what exists in nature; it embraces both the naturally existent and the nonexistent. This idea completely filled Tauler in all his considerations. We are told that an enlightened layperson, a "Friend of God from the Oberland," led him to this conviction. A mysterious story has been related concerning this. There are only conjectures about the place where this Friend of God lived; as to his identity, there are not even conjectures. He is said to have heard much about Tauler's manner of preaching and to have decided as a result to go to Tauler, who was then a preacher in Strasbourg, to fulfill a certain task pertaining to him. The relationship of Tauler to the Friend of God and the influence that the Friend had on him are described in a work that is printed together with the oldest editions of Tauler's sermons under the title *The Book of the Master.*[65] In this book, a Friend of God – in whom we recognize the same one who entered into relationship with Tauler – tells of a "master" whom one would recognize as Tauler himself. He tells how a revolution, a spiritual rebirth, had been brought about in a "master" and how this master, when he felt his death approaching, called the Friend to him and asked him to write the story of his "enlightenment" – taking care, however, that no one should ever discover the identity of the book's subject. He asks this because all the insights that emanate from him are in fact not his. "For know that God has performed everything through me, poor worm that I am, and thus it is not mine, but God's."[66]

A scholarly dispute has developed in connection with this matter, but it lacks any real significance. On the one hand (Heinrich Denifle, *The Writings of the Friend of God in the Oberland*), an attempt has been made to prove that the Friend of God never existed.[67] It is said that his existence was invented and that the books attributed to him in fact originated with someone else (Rulman Merswin). Wilhelm Preger (in his *History of German Mysticism*) has argued in support of his existence, the genuineness of the writings, and the correctness of the facts relating to Tauler.[68] It is not incumbent upon me to illuminate by obtrusive research this human relationship, which one who understands how to read the relevant writings will know full well is to remain a secret. (These relevant writings, among others, are: *Of a Self-Willed, Worldly Man Who Was Shown the Way to Humble Obedience by a Holy, Secular Priest*, 1338; *The Book of the Two Men*; *The Captured Knight*, 1349; *The Spiritual Stairs*, 1350; *Of the Spiritual Ladder*, 1357; *The Master Book*, 1369; *The Story of Two Young Fifteen-Year-Old Boys.*)[69]

It is enough to say of Tauler that at a certain stage of his life, a change such as the one I am about to describe took place in him. Here Tauler's personality is no longer in question, but rather a personality "in general." With regard to Tauler, we are concerned only with the fact that we must come to understand *his* transformation from the perspective indicated below. If we compare his later with his earlier activity, the fact of this transformation is immediately evident. I will leave aside all external circumstances and relate the inner soul processes of the "master" under the "influence of the layperson." What my readers think about the "master" and the "layperson" will depend on their spiritual dispositions; I cannot know if what I picture regarding them also comes into consideration for anyone else.

A master instructs his listeners about the relationship between the soul and universal being. He explains that the human being no longer feels that the natural, limited faculties of the individual personality are active within him when he descends into the profound depths of his soul. There it is no longer the individual who speaks, but God. There the human being does not see God or the world; God sees Himself. The human being has become *one* with God. But the master knows that this teaching has not yet come fully to life within him. He thinks it with the intellect, but he does not yet live within it with every fiber of his personality. In this way, he teaches about a state that he has not yet fully experienced within himself. The description of this state corresponds to the truth, but this truth is worth nothing if it does not acquire life, if it does not take up existence in the real world.

The "layperson," or "Friend of God," hears of the master and his teachings. He is not less permeated with the truth that the master utters than is the master himself. But he does not possess this truth as an intellectual idea – he possesses it as the whole force of his life. He knows that it is possible for one to speak of this truth when it is acquired from the outside, without living it in the least. In that case, one has nothing within oneself beyond the natural understanding of the intellect.

One then speaks of such natural understanding as though it were the highest truth, identical with the activity of universal being. This is not so, because it is not acquired in a life that approaches this knowledge as one already transformed and reborn. The knowledge one attains as a *merely* natural human being remains *merely* natural, even if one later verbally expresses the essential features of higher knowledge. The transformation must come from nature itself. Nature, which has evolved to a certain stage, must be evolved further by life; something new must come into existence through this further development. One must not simply look back to what has already taken place and consider as the highest truth what is *reproduced* in the mind concerning this development. One must instead *look forward* to what has not yet been created;

this knowledge must be the *beginning* of new meaning, not the *end* of the meaning of one's previous development.

Nature advances from worm to mammal, from mammal to human being in a real process, not a conceptual one. The human being is not intended merely to repeat this process in spirit. The spiritual recapitulation is only the beginning of a new development, which is also a spiritual reality. Then, human beings do not just understand what nature has produced; they carry nature further. They transform their understanding into living action. They bring forth the spirit within themselves, and from then on the spirit advances from one stage of development to another, just as nature advances. The spirit initiates a natural process on a higher level.

When one who has understood this evolution speaks about the God who sees Himself in the human being's inner life, this utterance assumes a different character. One attaches little value to the fact that a previously acquired insight has led into the depths of universal being; one's spiritual disposition acquires a new character. It continues to develop in the direction determined by universal being. Such a person not only *sees* the world differently; he *lives* life differently. He does not speak of the *meaning* that life already has by virtue of the forces and laws of the world; rather, he gives this life a new meaning.

As little as a fish bears within itself the mammal that appears at a later stage of evolution – just as little does the rational human being already harbor within him the higher human being that is still to be born. If a fish could understand itself and its surroundings, it would believe that its "fish-hood" represents the meaning of life. It would say, "The universal being is like a fish; universal being sees itself in the fish." The fish might speak in this way as long as it merely holds on firmly to its intellectual understanding. In reality, however, it does not hold on to it. In its actions, it goes beyond its understanding. It becomes a reptile and later a mammal. The meaning that the fish gives to itself goes beyond the meaning suggested to it by mere reflection. And this is how it must be for human beings. We give ourselves meaning; we do not stop at what we are and what we find reflected back to us. Understanding leaps beyond itself when it understands itself in the right way. Understanding cannot derive the world from a prefabricated god; it can only develop itself from a seed in a direction toward God.

Those who have come to this understanding choose not to view God as an external being. They want to treat God as a being who walks with them toward a goal that is just as mysterious at the outset as the nature of a mammal is to a fish. They do not want to simply know the hidden or self-revealing, already existing God; they want to be friends of the divine action and operation, which is superior to both existence and nonexistence. The layperson who came to the master was a "Friend of God" in this sense. Through him, the master was transformed from a contemplator of the nature of God into "one who lives in the spirit," one who did not merely contemplate but *lived* in the higher sense. The master no longer drew forth from within himself his intellectual concepts and ideas; these concepts and ideas sprang from him as living, existential spirit. He no longer merely edified his listeners; he moved them deeply. He no longer showed them the way within; he led them into a new life. This is related to us symbolically: We are told that during one of his sermons, forty people collapsed as though dead.

Another leader into such a new life is a certain work by an unknown author. It first became known when Martin Luther published it. The philologist Franz Pfeiffer recently reprinted it from a manuscript of 1497, with a translation in modern German facing the original text. The introduction to the work announces its intention and goal: "Here the Frankfurter says exceedingly deep and beautiful things of the consummate life." This introduction is followed by a "preface concerning the Frankfurter," which states:

> What is expressed in this booklet the omnipotent, eternal God has spoken through a wise, judicious, truthful, righteous man, His friend, who was formerly a Teutonic Knight, a priest, and a custodian in the house of the Teutonic Knights in Frankfurt. It teaches many lovely

insights into divine truth and especially how one can recognize the true and righteous Friends of God as well as the unrighteous, false, free spirits, who do much harm to the holy Church.[70]

"Free spirits" may be taken to mean those who live in a world of ideas like that of the above-described master before his transformation through the Friend of God. The "true and righteous Friends of God" are those who think in the way of the "layperson."

We can further ascribe to the book the intention of having the same effect on its readers as the "Friend of God from the Oberland" had upon the master. We do not know the author. But what does this mean? We do not know when he was born, when he died, nor what he did in ordinary life. It is integral to the way the author wanted to work that the facts of his outer life should remain forever secret. It is not the 'I' of this or that human being, born at a certain time, that is to speak to us, but that 'I'-hood on the basis of which the "uniqueness of the individuality" first develops (in the sense of the words of Paul Asmus; see above, pp. 29–30).

Imagine God receiving unto Himself all those who exist now and all those who have ever been, and in them becoming human; and imagine that they, too, become God in Him. If this did not also happen in me, then my fall and my estrangement would not be remedied until it indeed happened in me as well. And in this restoration and improvement, I can and

> should do nothing but only and purely submit to what is done, so that God alone accomplishes everything within me, and I yield to Him and all His works and His divine will. But if I do not want to become transformed, and instead cling to attributes of the self – that is, to "my" and "I," to "me" and so on – then God is hindered. He cannot accomplish His work within me, pure and alone and without obstacle. Accordingly, my fall and my estrangement remain unremedied.[71]

The "Frankfurter" does not intend to speak as an individual; he wishes to let God speak. Of course, he knows that he can do this only as a single, unique personality. But he is a Friend of God – that is, one who does not want to depict the nature of life through contemplation but wants to point out, through the living spirit, the *beginning* of a path of development.

The discussions in the book represent various instructions on how one can come to this path. The basic idea returns ever and again: the human being is to cast off everything connected with the outlook that allows him to appear as though he is an individual, separate personality. This idea seems to be carried out only with respect to the moral life; it can also readily be applied to the life of higher understanding. One should root out in oneself what appears as separateness. Then independent existence ceases; universal life enters us. We cannot take possession of this universal life by drawing it to us. It comes into us when we bring to silence the separate existence within us. We possess universal life least of all when we regard our individual existence as if universal life already reposed within it. It appears in individual existence only when this individual existence does not claim to be something.

The book calls this claim of individual existence the "assumption."[72] Through this assumption, the 'I' makes it impossible for universal life to enter it. The 'I' then puts itself in the place of the whole as a part, as something incomplete:

> The Perfect [*das Vollkommene*] is a being that comprises and embraces all beings in itself and in its essence; and without which, and outside of which, no true being exists; and within which all things have their being. For it is the being of all things, and is, in itself, unchangeable and immovable, and changes and moves all other things. But the separate and incomplete is that which issues forth from this Perfect, in the same way as the brilliance or luminosity emanating from the sun or from a light appears as something, as this or that. And this is known as "creature," and this separateness is not the Perfect. *Therefore, the Perfect is also not what is separate*. . . . When the Perfect comes, then one rejects what is separate. But when does it come? I say: when it is known, felt, and tasted in the soul, insofar as it is possible. For the lack is wholly in us, and not in it. For even though the sun illuminates the whole world, and even though it is as close to one person as to another, one who is blind nevertheless cannot see it. That is not a defect

> in the sun, but rather in the blind person. . . . If my eye is to see something, it must be cleansed of, or freed from, all other things. . . . Now, one might ask: Insofar as the Perfect is unknowable and incomprehensible for all creatures – and the soul is a creature – how can it be known in the soul?[73]

The answer is this: the creature is to be known *as creature*. This means that all creatures should be regarded as partaking in the quality of "having been created," and should not see themselves as an 'I' with selfhood. As a result, the above-described form of knowing is impossible. "In the creature in which the Perfect is to be known, 'creature-hood,' the quality of having been created, 'I,' selfhood, and everything of this nature must be lost and amount to nothing" (The writings of the "Frankfurter," chapter 1).[74] Thus, the soul must look into itself; there it will find its 'I'-being, or selfhood. If it stops there, it separates itself from the whole. If it regards its selfhood only as something as though loaned to it and obliterates this sense of selfhood in spirit, then the stream of universal life, of completeness [*Vollkommenheit*], will take hold of it.

> Let us say that a creature takes on something good, such as being, life, knowledge, insight, capacity – in other words, all that one would call good – and considers that it, as a creature, *is* that attribute or that the attribute belongs to it or is part of it. As long as this happens, such a creature rejects itself.[75]

> [There are] two eyes in the created soul of the human being. One has the possibility of looking into eternity, the other of looking into time and into the creature.[76]
>
> The human being should stand and exist in complete freedom, without self – that is, without selfhood, 'I'-hood, 'me,' 'mine,' 'my,' and qualities of this nature – so that he is as little concerned with seeking in all things himself, his opinion, and what belongs to him, as he would be if his self did not exist. And he should also hold little stock in himself, as if he did not exist, and as if someone else had accomplished all of his work.[77]

It must be understood that the concepts that the author of these words articulates through his higher ideas and feelings are those of a devout priest of his time. It is not a matter of the conceptual content but of the direction, not of the ideas but of the spiritual disposition. A person who does not live within Christian dogma (as this author does), but within the concepts of natural science, imbues those words with other thoughts. But with these other thoughts, those words still point in the same direction. And this direction is the one that leads to the overcoming of selfhood through selfhood itself. It is within the 'I' that the highest light shines for the human being. This light gives the right reflection to the world of ideas only when the human being is aware that it is not self-light but the universal light of the world. Consequently, there is no knowledge more important than self-knowledge, and at the same time, there is none that leads so completely beyond itself. When the 'I' knows itself in the right way, it is no longer an 'I.' In his language, the author of the work in question expresses it as follows:

> For God's nature is "without this and without that," without selfhood and 'I'-hood. But the nature and peculiarity of the creature is that it seeks and wants itself and what belongs to it, seeks and wants "this and that"; and from everything that it does or leaves undone, it wants to receive its own profit and advantage. But where the creature, or human being, loses his own being and selfhood and self, and goes beyond his self, there God enters with His own being; that is, with His selfhood.[78]

The human being ascends from a view of the 'I' that sees in it his own *being* to one where the 'I' appears as the organ in which universal being acts upon itself. Within the context of the writing we are considering, it is said: "If the human being can reach the point where he belongs as much to God as his hands belong to him, then he can rest content and seek no further."[79] This does not mean that one should stop at a certain point of development, but that, when one has come as far as these words indicate, one should no longer inquire into the meaning of the hand, but instead *use* the hand so that it serves the body to which it belongs.

Heinrich Suso and Jan van Ruysbroeck had a spiritual disposition that could be described as emotional genius. Their feelings were drawn almost instinctually to where Eckhart's and Tauler's feelings were led through a higher life of ideas. Suso's heart turns ardently toward a primal being that embraces the individual human being as well as the whole remaining world and in which, forgetting himself, he wants to be absorbed like a drop of water in the great ocean. He speaks of this yearning for universal being not as something he wants to grasp in his thoughts. He speaks of it as a natural impulse that intoxicates his soul with a desire for the annihilation of his separate existence and for rebirth in the all-embracing activity of infinite being:

> Turn your eyes toward being in its pure, plain simplicity, and thus let go of this or that partial aspect of being. Take "being" alone in itself, which is to be unmixed with nonbeing. For all nonbeing denies all being. Being, in itself, does the same: it denies all nonbeing. A thing that is yet to become or that has been – such a thing is not now in a state of essential presence. Now, one cannot recognize mixed being or nonbeing, except through a sense for the All-being. For if one wishes to understand a thing, then reason first encounters being and that is a being that brings forth all things. It is not a divided being of this or that creature, for divided being is all mixed together with some otherness of potential [*Anderheit einer Möglichkeit*] to receive something. Therefore the nameless divine being must be, in itself, an All-being that sustains all divided beings with its presence.[80]

Thus speaks Suso in the autobiography he composed in collaboration with his disciple Elsbet Stäglin. He, too, was a devout priest and lived fully in the Christian realm of ideas. He lived in it as if it were completely unthinkable for someone with his spiritual *orientation* to live in a different spiritual *world.* It is also true that one can recognize another meaning in his spiritual path. This speaks clearly of how the content of Christian teachings became an inner experience for him, of how his relationship with Christ became one between his spirit and eternal Truth in a manner of pure spiritual ideation. He wrote the *Little Book of Eternal Wisdom,*[81] in which he allowed "eternal Wisdom" to speak to its "servant," presumably himself:

> Don't you recognize me? How have you sunk so low – or has your consciousness vanished through sorrows of the heart, my delicate child? It is I, merciful Wisdom, who have opened wide the depths of bottomless compassion – which remains hidden, even to all the saints – to receive you and all repentant hearts in kindness. It is I, sweet, eternal Wisdom, who became poor and outcast so that I might restore you to your worthiness. It is I, who suffered bitter death, in order that I might give rise to life in you again! Here I stand, pale and bloody and loving, as I stood by the high gallows of the Cross, between you and the stern judgment of my Father. It is I, your Brother; it is I, your Bridegroom. I will utterly forget everything you have ever done against me, as though it had never happened, if

> you now completely turn to me and never again separate yourself from me.[82]

As we can see, everything material and temporal in the Christian view of the world has become for Suso a spiritual, ideal process within his soul. From some chapters of the autobiography of Suso, it could appear as if he had let himself be led not by the mere activity of his own spiritual faculties but by external revelations, by spirit-like visions. But he clearly expresses his opinion about this: one attains the truth only by the exercise of reason, not through revelation:

> I also wish to tell you . . . of the difference between pure truth and dubious visions originating in professions of faith. Direct beholding of the unadorned Divinity: this is pure, genuine truth free of all doubt. And for every vision, the more grounded in reason and free of images it is, and the more akin to this same unadorned beholding, the nobler it is.[83]

Meister Eckhart likewise leaves no doubt that he rejects the view that would see the spirit in physical-spatial forms, in apparitions that can be perceived in the same way as sensory ones. Spirits like Suso and Eckhart are opponents of a view such as that expressed in the spiritualism that developed in the eighteenth century.

Jan van Ruysbroeck, the Belgian mystic, walked the same paths as Suso. His spiritual path found a spirited opponent in Jean de Gerson (born 1363), who was for some time chancellor of the University of Paris and who played an important role at the Council of Constance. It throws light on the nature of the mysticism cultivated by Tauler, Suso, and Ruysbroeck if one compares it with the mystical endeavors of Gerson, whose predecessors were Richard of St. Victor, Bonaventura, and others. Ruysbroeck himself fought against those whom he counted among the heretical mystics. He believed heretical mystics to be all those who, on the basis of an unconsidered intellectual judgment, hold all things to be the emanation of *one* primal being and who thus see in the world only a diversity and in God the unity of that diversity.

Ruysbroeck did not count himself among those mystics. He knew that one cannot reach the primordial essence by contemplating the things themselves, but only by ascending from this lower to a higher way of thinking. He also opposed those who wished to discover spontaneously in the individual human being, in our separate existence – the human being as creature – our higher nature. He very much lamented the error that eliminates all differences in the sensory world and says lightly that things merely appear to be different, whereas, in fact, they are all essentially the same.

For a way of thinking such as Ruysbroeck's, this would be the same as if one were to say, "It is of no concern to us that our eyes see trees along an avenue converge in the distance. The fact is that they remain equally distant, and so our eyes must adjust in order to see them correctly." But our eyes do see correctly. The trees do converge owing to a necessary law of nature, and we should not complain about the way we see but understand in *spirit* why we see *in this way.*

Mystics also do not turn away from objects of the senses. They accept them as sensory, as they are. And it is clear to them that such phenomena do not change based on any intellectual judgment. But in the spirit, the mystics go beyond the senses and reason, and only then do they find unity. They have an unshakable *faith* that they can develop themselves to the point of seeing this unity. Therefore they ascribe to human nature the divine spark that can be brought to *shine within on its own.*

It is different with Gerson's kind. They *do not* believe in this inner, self-shining light. For them, what human beings can see always remains an external reality that must approach them outwardly from one side or another. Ruysbroeck believed that the highest wisdom must become apparent to mystical vision; Gerson believed only that the soul could illuminate the content of an external teaching (that of the Church). Gerson saw mysticism as merely having a warm feeling for everything that is revealed in this teaching. To Ruysbroeck, it was a belief that the content of this teaching is also born in the soul. Gerson reproves Ruysbroeck for imagining not only that he possesses the capacity to see universal being with clarity, but also that an activity of universal being manifests itself in this vision.

Gerson could not understand Ruysbroeck. They were speaking of two different things. Ruysbroeck has his eye fixed on the life of the soul that lives into its god; Gerson sees only a life of the soul that wants to love a god who it will never be able to live within. Like so many others, Gerson, too, fought against a foreign idea only because he did not have the experience needed to understand it.[b]

[b] See addendum II, p. 171.

.III.

CARDINAL NICHOLAS OF CUSA

Nicholas Chrypffs of Cusa (1401–1464) was a gloriously shining star in the firmament of medieval spiritual life. He stood at the pinnacle of the knowledge of his time. He produced outstanding work in mathematics. In natural science, he may be described as the precursor to Copernicus, for he believed that the earth is a moving heavenly body like other heavenly bodies. He had broken with the view that the great astronomer Tycho Brahe still held a hundred years later when Brahe argued against the teaching of Copernicus by saying, "The earth is a coarse and heavy mass, unsuited for movement. How can Copernicus make a star of it and lead it around in the atmosphere?"[84] Nicholas of Cusa, who not only embraced the knowledge of his time but developed it further, also had to a high degree the capacity to awaken this knowledge to inner life. He thus enabled it not only to elucidate the external world but also to mediate for the human being the spiritual life for which he must yearn from the most profound depths of his soul.

If we compare Nicholas with such spirits as Eckhart or Tauler, we reach an important conclusion. Nicholas is the scientific thinker whose goal is to rise to a higher view through his research into world phenomena; Eckhart and Tauler are the believing confessors who seek a higher life through the meaning contained in their faith. Nicholas finally reaches the same inner life as Meister Eckhart, but the substance of his inner life is rich with knowledge. The full meaning of the difference becomes clear when we consider that for a person who is engaged in the various sciences, there is a real danger of misjudging the scope of the paths to knowledge in different fields of learning. Such a person can easily be misled into the belief that there is only one way of knowing, and will then either overestimate or underestimate this path of knowledge and how it leads to results in the various sciences.

In the one case, he will approach phenomena of the highest spiritual life in the same way as a problem in physics, and deal with them in terms of concepts used to elucidate the forces of gravity and electricity. According to whether he considers himself to be more or less enlightened, the world becomes a blindly acting mechanism, an organism, the functional construction of a personal god, or, perhaps, a structure directed and penetrated by a more or less clearly imagined "world soul." In the other case, he notices that the particular knowledge of which he has experience is useful only for the things of the sensory world. Then he becomes a skeptic who might say to himself, "We cannot know anything about what lies beyond the sensory world. Our knowledge has limits. When we aspire to the necessities of higher life, we merely throw ourselves into the arms of faith, untouched by knowledge." For a learned theologian like Nicholas of Cusa, who was at the same time a natural scientist, the second danger was particularly real. In his education, he was a product of Scholasticism, the dominant philosophy in the scholarly life of the Church of the Middle Ages, which had been brought to its highest flowering by Thomas Aquinas (1225–1274), the "Prince of Scholastics." This philosophy must be used as a background if one wants to depict the personality of Nicholas of Cusa.

Scholasticism is absolutely a product of human ingenuity. Logic celebrated its greatest triumphs in Scholasticism. One who aims to elaborate concepts in their sharpest and clearest contours should serve an apprenticeship with the Scholastics. It is they who provide the best training for the technique of thinking. They had an incomparable agility in the field of pure thought. It is easy to underestimate what they were capable of in this field. In most areas of learning, pure thought is difficult to achieve. Most people attain it clearly only in the areas of counting and calculating (arithmetic) and in considering the properties of geometric forms. We can count by adding a unit to a number in our thoughts, without having to rely on sensory images. We also calculate without such images, in the pure element of thought alone. As for geometric forms, we know that they do not completely coincide with any sensory image. In the reality of the senses, there exists no (ideal) circle. And yet our thinking occupies itself with this circle.

It is more difficult to find conceptual counterparts for objects and processes that are more complicated than numerical and spatial structures. This difficulty has led, in various fields of investigation, to the claim that real knowledge is represented only by that which can be measured and counted. This is decidedly wrong in that it is one-sided, but it seduces many, as often only one-sided ideas can. The truth is that most people are not capable of grasping the purely conceptual when it no longer applies to things that can be measured or counted. But someone who cannot grasp the higher realms of life and knowledge resembles a child who has not yet learned to count in any other way than by adding one pea to another. The thinker who said that there is as much true knowledge in any field of learning as there is mathematics in it did not grasp the full truth of the matter. We must require that everything that cannot be measured and counted is treated in the same conceptual fashion as numerical and spatial structures. And this requirement was greatly respected by the Scholastics. They sought the conceptual content of things everywhere, just as the mathematician seeks it in measuring and counting.

In spite of this accomplished logical skill, the Scholastics attained only a one-sided and subordinate concept of cognition. According to this concept, in the process of cognition, the human being produces an image of what is to be grasped. It is evident that with such a concept of cognition, one must place all reality outside cognition. In the process of cognition one cannot grasp a thing itself but *only an image* of this thing. One also cannot grasp oneself in self-knowledge; what one grasps is only an image of the self. It is quite in the spirit of Scholasticism that someone who is closely acquainted with it says:

> In time, the human being has no perception of his 'I,' the hidden foundation of his spiritual being and life. . . . He will . . . never come to the point of being able to look at himself; for either, forever estranged from God, he will find in himself only a bottomless dark abyss, an endless emptiness – or else, blessed in God, he will turn his gaze inward, finding only God, whose sun of grace shines within him and whose *image* is reflected in the spiritual traits of his being. (K. Werner, *Francisco Suárez and the Scholasticism of the Last Centuries*)[85]

Whoever thinks about all knowing in this way only has a concept of *that form* of knowing that applies to the things of the external world. The sense-perceptible aspects of something always remain external to us. This is why we can internalize the outer sense-perceptible world only in the form of pictures. When we perceive a color or a stone, we cannot become them in order to know the being of color or the being of stone. Neither can the color or the stone transform itself into a part of our own being! Seeing as though this form of cognition focuses on the outer aspect of things, we can ask: Is a concept of this form of cognition exhaustive? It is true that, for Scholasticism, all human cognition coincides *essentially* with *this* form of cognition. Another writer who is very familiar with Scholasticism (Otto Willmann, *History of Idealism*) characterizes the concept of cognition related to this orientation of thought in the following way:[86]

> Our spirit, which in earthly life is joined to the body, is primarily directed toward the surrounding physical world. But it focuses on the spirit in the world: the essences, natures, and forms of things, the elements of existence that are akin to it and that provide it with the rungs by which it ascends to the suprasensory. The field of our cognition is therefore the realm of experience; but we should learn to understand what it offers, penetrate to its sense and its thoughts, and thereby open ourselves to the world of thought.

The Scholastic was not able to come to a different concept of cognition. His theological dogmas prevented him from doing so. If he had fixed his spiritual gaze upon what he regarded as a mere image, he would have observed that the spiritual meaning of things reveals itself in this so-called image. He would then have found that God is not merely *mirrored* within his own inner life, but that He *lives* in this inner life, has an essential presence there. In looking within, he would not have stared at a dark abyss of endless emptiness, nor at a mere image of God;

instead, he would have felt that a life pulses within him, which is the Divine Life itself; and that his own life is indeed God's life. This, the Scholastic could not acknowledge. In his opinion, God could not enter into him and speak from within him; He could be in him only as an image.

In reality, it had to be assumed that the Divinity exists outside the self. God must *reveal* Himself through supernatural communications from outside and cannot do so within, through the spiritual life. This kind of thinking is least effective in achieving what is striven for – that is, the most sublime possible concept of the Divinity. Rather, this kind of thinking reduces the Divinity to a thing among other things – the only difference being that aspects of the world reveal themselves to the human being through experience, whereas the Divinity is thought to reveal Himself in a supernatural way. For the Scholastic, the difference between knowledge of the Divine and knowledge of the created world is that, in the case of the latter, objects are present in the experienced world; thus one comes to gain *knowledge* about them. In the case of the Divine, the object cannot be experienced; one achieves knowledge of it only through *faith*.

For the Scholastics, therefore, the highest realities were not objects of reason, but only objects of faith. According to the Scholastic view, however, the relationship of reason to faith is not such that in one field, *only* reason holds sway, and in another, *only* faith:

> Cognition of what exists is possible for us because it originates in a generative insight. Things are *for* the spirit because they are *from* the spirit; they have something to say to us because they have a meaning that has been bestowed upon them from a higher intelligence. (O. Willmann, *History of Idealism*)[87]

Since God has created the world according to His ideas, when we grasp the ideas of the world through scientific reflection, we can also grasp the traces of Divinity in the world. But we can only know the essential nature of God through supernatural revelation, which requires faith. The way we think about the highest realities is decided not by human reason but by faith, and "to faith belongs everything contained in the scriptures of the New and Old Covenant and in the divine traditions" (Joseph Kleutgen, *The Theology of Antiquity*).[88] We cannot take on the task here of describing in detail and pursuing an explanation of the relationship between beliefs based on faith and those based on reason.

Beliefs, the content of faith, have their origin in inner human experience. They are preserved and passed on with no consciousness of how they originated. It is claimed that they came into the world through supernatural revelation. Christian beliefs were simply accepted by the Scholastics as tradition. Science and inner experience were not allowed to claim any rights over them. Scholastics could no more permit themselves to create a concept of God than scientists could create a tree;

they had to accept the revealed concept as given, just as natural scientists accept the tree as given. The Scholastic could never admit that spirit itself shines and lives within. Consequently, he established a boundary for the jurisdiction of science at the point where the field of outer experience ends. Human cognition could not be permitted to produce a concept of the higher entities on its own. It chose to accept a revealed one. The Scholastics could not concede that by accepting traditional beliefs, they in fact embraced what had been brought forth at an earlier stage of human spiritual life and declared it to be a revelation.

In the course of the development of Scholasticism, all the ideas that still pointed toward the way human beings bring forth concepts of Divinity in a natural manner disappeared. During the first centuries of the emergence of Christianity, at the time of the Church fathers, we see how, bit by bit, theological doctrine came into being through the inclusion of inner experiences. John Scotus Eriugena, who stood at the height of Christian theological learning in the ninth century, still spoke of theological insight as a thoroughly inner experience. Among the Scholastics of the succeeding centuries, this quality of inner experience is completely lost; the old doctrines are reinterpreted as external, supernatural revelation. Thus one can interpret the activity of the mystical theologians Eckhart, Tauler, Suso, and their companions by saying that they were inspired by the reinterpreted theological teachings of the Church to bring forth similar insight through their own inner experience.

* * *

Nicholas of Cusa began the task of ascending from the knowledge one acquires in the various sciences to inner experience itself. There can be no doubt that the excellent technique of logic that the Scholastics had developed (and in which Nicholas had been educated) furnished a superb means of attaining inner experiences, even though the Scholastics themselves were kept from this road by the strength of their faith. But we can only fully understand Nicholas by realizing that his vocation as a priest, which raised him to the position of cardinal, prevented him from breaking completely with the faith of the Church, whose contemporary expression was found in Scholastic theology. We find him so far advanced along a certain path that each additional step would have led him, of necessity, away from the Church. Consequently, we understand the cardinal best if we complete that step that he did not take and then, in retrospect, illuminate what he had intended.

The most important concept of the spiritual life articulated by Nicholas is that of "learned ignorance." By "learned ignorance," he means a form of cognition that stands above what is represented by ordinary knowledge. Ordinary knowledge is based on the comprehension of an object through the spirit. The most important characteristic of knowledge is that it gives information about an entity outside spirit – that is, knowledge addresses what spirit itself is not. In knowledge, the spirit is occupied with matters considered to be outside itself. But what the spirit forms in itself concerning objects of the outer world is their *essence*. Things *are* spirit. At first, the human being sees the spirit only through the sheath in which it appears in the sense world. What remains outside the spirit is only this sense-perceptible sheath; the essence of the thing enters into the spirit.

When spirit views this essence – which is the substance of its own substance – it can no longer speak of knowledge. It does not observe an object that is outside itself; it looks upon a thing that is part of itself. It looks upon itself. It no longer knows; it only observes itself. It is not engaged in "knowing" but in "*not knowing*." It no longer *grasps* something through spirit; it "beholds, without grasping,"[89] its own life. The highest level of cognition, in relation to the lower levels, is "not knowing." But it is clear that the *essence* of things can be communicated only at this level of understanding.

With his "learned not knowing," Nicholas of Cusa therefore speaks of nothing other than knowledge reborn as inner experience. He himself tells of how he came to this inner experience:

> I made many attempts to unite the thoughts about God and the world, about Christ and the Church, into one fundamental idea. But none

> satisfied me until finally, during my return from Greece by sea, the gaze of my spirit lifted, as if through an inspiration from on high, to the view in which God appeared to me as the highest unity of all contrasts.[90]

Nicholas's predecessors more or less played a role in this inspiration. In his mode of thinking, one recognizes a unique renewal of the ideas we encounter in the writings of a certain Dionysius. The above-mentioned John Scotus Eriugena translated these writings into Latin. He called the author the "great and divine revealer." These writings first came to light in the first half of the sixth century. They were ascribed to Dionysius the Areopagite, who is mentioned in the Acts of the Apostles and was converted to Christianity by Paul. We shall not go into the question of when these writings were really composed. Their content had a strong effect on Nicholas, as it had likewise on John Scotus Eriugena; and it must also have been a stimulus for the way of thinking of Eckhart and his companions. The "learned not knowing" is, in a certain way, prefigured in these writings. Here we shall record only the main characteristic of the thinking inherent in these writings.

Initially, human beings learn to know the things of the sensory realm. They reflect on the existence and activity of these things. The primal ground [*Urgrund*] of all things must exist in a higher realm than the things themselves. We cannot, therefore, expect to comprehend it with the same concepts and ideas with which we comprehend the things themselves. If people attribute to the primal ground (God) qualities they have come to know within the sensory realm, such qualities can only be mental crutches for the weak spirit, which draws the primal ground down to its own level in order to picture it. In truth, no quality possessed by lower phenomena can be said to belong to God. It cannot even be said that God *is*. "Being" is also a mental image that human beings have formed in connection with lower phenomena. God is exalted above "being" and "not being."

The god to whom we ascribe qualities is not the true one. We arrive at the true god if we imagine a "Supra-God" above the god to whom we attribute such qualities. We can know nothing of this "Supra-God" in the ordinary sense. To reach such a god, "knowing" must flow into "unknowing." We can see that such a view is based on the awareness that the human being can, in a purely natural way, develop a higher form of cognition through what he acquires through the sciences – a form of cognition which is no longer a *mere knowing*. The Scholastic view declared knowledge to be powerless to undergo such a development, and, at the point where knowledge is supposed to end, allows faith, based on external revelation, to come to the aid of knowledge. Nicholas of Cusa was on the way toward once again developing from out of knowledge *that* which the Scholastics had declared unreachable for cognition.

From the point of view of Nicholas of Cusa, we cannot say that there is only *one* kind of knowing. On the contrary, on the one hand we have a knowing that mediates knowledge of what exists around us, while on the other hand we have a knowing that is identical with the object we are trying to understand. The former predominates in the sciences as the knowledge we acquire about the objects and processes of the sensory world; the latter is within us when we *live* in the knowledge that has been acquired. The second kind of comprehension develops from the first. Yet it is the same world to which both refer, and it is the same human being who partakes in both. The question must follow: How does it happen that one and the same person develops two ways of knowing the same world? The direction in which the answer is to be sought is already indicated with Tauler (see pp. 67–70). With Nicholas of Cusa, this answer can form itself in an even more decisive way.

Initially, the human being lives as a separate (individual) being among other separate beings. In addition to the ways these beings affect one another, the faculty of (lower) cognition is found in the individual human being. Through the senses, he receives impressions of other beings and works through those impressions with his spiritual faculties. He directs his spiritual gaze away from external things and contemplates himself, his own activity. In this way, self-knowledge arises within him. As long as he remains at this level of self-knowledge, he does not yet see himself in the true sense of the word. He can maintain the belief that there is some hidden entity at work within him, and that what appears to be *his own* activity is only the expressions and actions of this other entity.

Then there may come the moment when the human being understands – through an indisputable inner experience – that what he perceives and encounters within himself is not the manifestation or activity of a hidden force or entity but, instead, that entity itself in its purest form. He may then say, "I encounter all other things as, in a certain sense, complete, and I, standing outside them, bring to them what the spirit has to say about them. But I myself live in that which I bring to these things from within myself; that is me; that is my own being."

What speaks there in the depths of my spirit? It is the knowledge I have acquired about the things of the world. But it is not some effect or manifestation that speaks. What speaks holds back nothing of what is present in it. In *this* knowledge, the world speaks in all its immediacy. But I have acquired this knowledge from the world and from myself, as a being among other beings. From the depths of my own being, both I and the world speak. I no longer express merely my own nature; I express the nature of things. My 'I' is the form, the organ, through which the things of the world speak their own true nature. I have realized that it is my own being that

I experience within; this experience widens for me into another: In me and through me, universal being expresses itself or, in other words, knows itself. Now I can no longer feel that I am merely a thing among things; I can sense that I am a form in which universal being has its life.

Consequently, it is only natural that one and the same person should have two ways of knowing. With regard to sensory facts, the human being is a thing among things, and, as such, attains knowledge of these things. At any moment, however, a person can have the higher experience that he is the form in which universal being sees itself. Then he himself is transformed from an entity among other entities into a form of universal being – and with this transformation, the knowledge of things becomes the expression of the nature of things. This transformation can only be accomplished by the human being himself. The content of higher cognition does not exist until this level of cognition is reached. Only in creating this form of higher cognition does the human being achieve the quality of essential being, and only through this higher form of human cognition do the things of the sense world bring their essential being into actual existence.

Limiting higher levels of cognition to the mere expression of what already exists outside in the sense world really means renouncing all higher cognition. Given the fact that, as part of the sense-perceptible world, the human being is a thing among things and attains higher cognition only when, as a sensory being, he transforms himself into a higher being, it follows that he can never replace the one form of cognition with the other. Rather, human spiritual life is made up of a perpetual back-and-forth movement between two poles of cognition, between *knowing* and *seeing*. If the human being were to shut himself off from seeing, he would forgo the essential nature of things. If he were to shut himself off from sensory knowing, he would deprive himself of the things whose essential nature he wants to understand. The same things reveal themselves to both sensory cognition and to the higher seeing: to the former in terms of their external appearance, and to the latter in terms of their inner being. It is not inherent in the nature of things that, at a certain stage, they appear only as external objects. This happens because the human being must first transform himself to the point where the things of the world cease to have only an external reality.

It is only with these considerations in mind that certain views elaborated by natural science during the nineteenth century appear in their proper light. Adherents of those views would say: We hear, see, and touch the things of the material world through the senses. The eye, for example, communicates a light phenomenon – a color. We say that a body gives off *red* light when, through the medium of our eyes, we experience the sensation "red." But in other cases, the eye gives us another sensation. If the eye is struck or pressed, or if an electric current passes through the head, then the eye experiences a sensation of light. When we have the sensation that a body gives off a certain color of light, something may be happening in that body that does not in any way resemble color. Regardless of what is occurring in the outer world, as long as the process can make an impression upon the eye, a sensation of color arises. Our perception arises in us because our organs are constituted in a certain way. Occurrences in the outer world remain outside us; we know only the *effects* that external processes produce within us.

Hermann Helmholtz (1821–1894) expressed this idea in a clearly defined way:

> Our sensations are effects produced in our organs by external causes. The way those effects manifest depends substantially on the kind of apparatus they encounter. Insofar as the quality of our sensations provides information about the specific nature of the external stimulus, one may consider these to be *signs* [*Zeichen*] of the stimulus but not a *likeness* of it. We require a picture to be in some way similar to the object represented. We likewise require similarity of form in a statue; a similarity of perspective in the field of view of a drawing; and, in addition to the perspective, a similarity of colors in a painting. But a sign need bear no resemblance to the external object. The relationship between the two is limited: the same object, given the same circumstances, must evoke the same sign. Accordingly, unlike signs always correspond to

> unlike stimuli. . . . If in the course of ripening, berries of a certain variety develop both a red pigment and sugar, then red color and sweet taste will always be found together in the sensations brought about by berries of this kind. (See Helmholtz, *The Facts in Perception.*)[91]

I have described this kind of thinking in detail in my *Philosophy of Spiritual Activity* and in my *Riddles of Philosophy.*

Let us follow step by step the train of thought adopted by this view. A process is assumed to occur in the outer world. It produces an effect on my sensory organ; my nervous system transmits the resulting impression to my brain, and another process is produced there. I now have the sensation "red." It is said that, therefore, the sensation of the color red is not outside of me but within me. All our sensations are only *signs* of external processes, the true nature of which we know nothing. We live within our sensations and know nothing of their origin. In line with this way of thinking, we can also say that, if we had no eyes, there would be no color. Nothing would then transform the external process, which is unknown to us, into the sensation "red."

This train of thought is, for many people, seductive. Nevertheless, it is based on a complete misinterpretation of the facts under consideration. (If many contemporary natural scientists and philosophers were not seriously deluded by this way of thinking, then one could speak about it less often. But this delusion has, in fact, corrupted contemporary thinking in many ways.) Because the human being is a thing among other things, the things of the world must make an impression upon him if he is to discover anything about them. A process outside the human being must give rise to a process within the human being if "red" is to appear in the field of vision. One must only ask: What is outside, and what is inside? Outside is a process in space and time. Inside there is certainly a similar process. Such a process commences in the eye and continues on into the brain when I perceive "red." I cannot directly observe the process that takes place "inside" any more than I can directly perceive in the "outer" world the motion of light waves, which physicists believe corresponds to the color "red." It is only in this sense, however, that I can speak of "outside" and "inside." Differentiating between "outside" and "inside" is only valid at the level of *sensory cognition*. This leads me to assume a spatiotemporal process in the "outer" world, though I cannot perceive it *directly*. Moreover, it also leads me to assume that such a process exists within me, which I am also unable to perceive directly. But I also assume other spatiotemporal processes in ordinary life, which I cannot perceive directly. For example, I hear a piano played in the next room and assume that a human being having spatial dimensions sits at the piano and plays. My way of representing matters to myself is the same, whether I speak of processes *within* me or *outside* me. I assume that the characteristics of such processes are analogous to qualities of those processes perceived by my senses, but that, for certain reasons, they are inaccessible to my direct observation.

If I were to deny to these processes all the characteristics that my senses reveal to me in the realm of space and time, it would be like the proverbial knife without a handle whose blade is missing. Therefore, all I can say is that spatiotemporal processes take place in the "outer" world and that they give rise to spatiotemporal processes "within." Both are necessary if "red" is to appear in my field of vision. In as much as it is not spatiotemporal, it would be useless to look for this red, whether "outside" or "inside." The natural scientists and philosophers who cannot find red in the "outer" world should also not attempt to look for it "within." It is not "inside" in the same sense that it is not "outside." To say that everything the sensory world presents to us is really an inner world of sensations, and to look for something external that corresponds to it, is an impossible notion. Consequently, we cannot say that red, sweet, hot, and so on are but *signs* that arise within us, excited by something very different in the outer world. In fact, the effect produced *within us* as the result of an external process is completely different from what appears in the field of our perception.

If we want to refer to what arises *in us* as "signs," we can say that these signs appear within our organism in order to communicate perceptions that, in their immediacy, are neither inside nor outside us. Rather, they belong to that common world to which my "external" world and my "interior" world both belong. If I wish to grasp that common realm, I must rise to the higher level of cognition for which this dichotomy no longer exists.

(I am well aware that those who accept as gospel the view that our entire world of experience is made up of sensations of unknown origin will look down their noses at this exposition, as does Dr. Erich Adikes, who, in his work *Kant contra Haeckel*, says condescendingly: "For the time being, people like Haeckel and thousands of his kind philosophize merrily away, completely unconcerned with theories of cognition or with critical introspection."[92] Such gentlemen have no idea of the insignificance of *their own* theories of cognition. They suspect a lack of critical introspection only in others. We shall not begrudge them their "wisdom.")

Nicholas of Cusa has excellent ideas on exactly the point we are considering. By maintaining a clear separation between the lower and higher forms of cognition, he gains extensive insight into the fact that the human being, as a sensory being, experiences *within himself* only those processes that, as effects, must be unlike the corresponding *external* processes. On the other hand, this differentiation between the two forms of cognition keeps Nicholas from confusing those inner processes with the realities that appear in our field of perception, and that, in their immediacy, are neither outside nor inside, but are elevated above such disparity.

Nicholas was "prevented by his priestly cloth" from following unreservedly the path that this insight indicated to him.[93] We see him making a good beginning with the progression from "knowing" to "not knowing," but, at the same time, we must note that in the field of "not knowing" he has nothing to impart except the theological teachings offered to us by Scholasticism.

Admittedly, he does know how to develop this theology brilliantly. His teachings on providence, Christ, Creation, the Redemption of humanity, and the moral life are completely in harmony with Christian dogma. In keeping with his spiritual direction, he might have said, "I am confident that human nature, having immersed itself in every science, can out of itself transform 'knowing' into a 'not-knowing' that satisfies the conditions of higher cognition." In this case, he would have rejected (which he did not) the traditional ideas of soul, immortality, Redemption, God, Creation, the Trinity, and so on, and would have upheld those that he himself had discovered.

Nicholas, however, was so immersed in Christian concepts that he could easily believe he was awakening his own inner "not-knowing," whereas he was, in fact, merely presenting the traditional views of his education. He was, however, standing before a fateful abyss in human spiritual life. He was a *scientifically-minded* person. Science initially removes the human being from an innocent concord with the world, which exists as long as he gives himself to life in naïve purity. With such a disposition toward life, the human being dimly feels his connection to the universe as a whole. He is, like other beings, woven into the stream of the workings of nature. With knowledge, he separates himself from this whole. He creates a spiritual world within himself. With this, he confronts nature in solitude. He has become richer, but this wealth is a burden that he bears with difficulty. For it initially weighs upon him alone. He must, out of his own strength, find the way back to nature. He must understand that now he has to integrate his wealth into the stream of universal workings, just as nature had previously integrated his poverty. It is here that all evil demons lie in wait for the human being, whose strength can easily grow weary. Instead of bringing about this integration himself, in his weariness he takes refuge in a revelation coming from outside, which delivers him from his loneliness and directs the knowledge that he experiences as a burden back to the primordial origin of existence, to the Divinity. He will think, as did Nicholas of Cusa, that he is walking his own path, while in reality, he finds only the path that his spiritual development has shown him.

There are essentially three paths that one can

take when one arrives at the point Nicholas had reached. One is *positive faith*, which comes to us from outside. The second is *despair*, when one stands alone with one's burden and feels the entirety of existence grow tenuous. The third path is the development of the deepest, self-willed forces of the human being. *Trust* in the world must be one guide along this third path; the *courage* to follow this trust wherever it leads must be the other.[c]

[c] See addendum III, p. 171.

.IV.

AGRIPPA OF NETTESHEIM AND THEOPHRASTUS PARACELSUS

Heinrich Cornelius Agrippa of Nettesheim (1486–1535) and Theophrastus Paracelsus (1493–1541) followed the path set out by Nicholas of Cusa's way of thinking. They immersed themselves in nature and, as comprehensively as possible, endeavored to explore its laws with all the means available at the time. In this knowledge of nature, they also saw the true foundation for all higher cognition. They sought to develop this foundation themselves out of natural science by allowing science to be reborn in the spirit.

Agrippa of Nettesheim led an eventful life. He was born in Cologne, the descendant of a noble family. He studied medicine and jurisprudence at an early age and informed himself about natural phenomena as was then customary within certain circles and societies, as well as through contact with several scholars who carefully kept secret whatever insights they gained into nature. To that end, he repeatedly went to Paris, Italy, and England, and he also visited the well-known Abbot Trithemius of Sponheim in Würzburg. He taught in scientific institutions at various times, and occasionally entered the services of the rich and noble, at whose disposal he placed his talents as a statesman and scientist. His biographers describe the services he rendered as not always above reproach, and it is said that he acquired money under the pretext of being adept in secret arts and secured various advantages for people by means of these arts. If this is true, it is countered by his unmistakable and ceaseless urge to honestly acquire the entire scope of the learning of his time and to deepen this knowledge in the spirit of a higher form of cognition. He strove to gain clarity concerning both natural science and higher cognition. Only one who has insight into the ways by which one achieves these two forms of cognition can attain such a goal.

Just as it is true that natural science must finally be lifted into the realm of spirit before it can lead to higher cognition, it is also true that if it is to provide the right foundation for a higher level of understanding, it must, initially, remain within its own domain. "Spirit in nature" is present only for spirit. As surely as nature is in this sense spiritual, it is equally certain that nothing perceived in nature by physical organs is directly spiritual. Nothing that is spirit can appear to my eye as spirit. I must *not* seek spirit as spirit in nature. This happens when I immediately interpret a process of the outer world in a spiritual way, as when, for example, I ascribe to plants a soul that is only remotely analogous to the human soul. I also do this when I ascribe a spatial or temporal existence to spirit or to soul itself – when, for example, I say of the eternal human soul that it lives in time without the body, but still in the manner of a body, rather than as pure spirit. And I do this when I believe that the spirit of a deceased person can show itself in some sort of sense-perceptible manifestation.

Forms of spiritualism that commit this error merely show that they have not understood the true nature of spirit, but simply desire to perceive spirit directly as a crude, sensory manifestation. This is a misunderstanding of the nature of both the senses and the spirit. Spiritualism de-spiritualizes the ordinary sensory phenomena, which occur hour after hour before our eyes, in order to address something rare, surprising, and unusual as though it were spirit. There is a failure to understand that for someone with the capacity to see the spirit, what lives as "spirit in nature" reveals itself, for example, in the collision of two elastic spheres. This revelation is not limited to processes that are enticing because of their unusual nature and the fact that they cannot be immediately understood in their natural context.

The spiritualist, however, also draws the spirit down into a lower sphere. He does not explain spatial phenomena perceived by the senses by means of those forces and beings that are, in turn, spatial and available to the senses; rather, he resorts to "spirits," which he then equates fully with what the senses perceive. This way of thinking is based on an insufficient capacity to comprehend spirit. One is incapable of viewing spirit in a manner consistent with its nature, and thus one satisfies a need for spirit by staying within mere sense experience. The spirit shows no spirit to such people; therefore, they look for it through the senses. Just as they see clouds sailing through the air, so they want to see spirits hurrying along.

Agrippa of Nettesheim fought for a truly natural science that does not attempt to explain natural phenomena through spiritual beings haunting the world of the senses, but instead, sees *only* what is natural in nature and only what is spiritual in spirit. Of course, it would be a complete misunderstanding of Agrippa to compare *his* natural science with that of later centuries, which has at its disposal completely different experiences. Through such a comparison, it could easily appear that he still attributes to the direct activity of spirits what in fact has its cause only in natural circumstances or erroneous experiences. Moritz Carrière does him this injustice when he says (though not with ill will):

> Agrippa gives a long list of the things that belong to the sun, the moon, the planets, or the fixed stars, and that receive their influences. For instance, related to the sun are fire, blood, laurel, gold, topaz; they bestow the gift of the sun's courage, serenity, and light. . . . The animals have a sense of nature that, more exalted than human reason, approaches the spirit of prophecy. . . . People can be made to love and hate, to become sick and healthy. Thus one

> casts a spell upon thieves that prohibits them from stealing, prohibits merchants from trading, prohibits ships and mills from motion, and prevents lightning from striking. This is done with potions, salves, images, rings, and charms; the blood of hyenas or dragons is suitable for this purpose. *One is reminded of Shakespeare's cauldron of the witches.*[94]

No, one is *not* reminded of it, if one understands Agrippa correctly. He did, of course, believe what was thought to be incontrovertible during his time. But we also do this today with regard to what is considered "factual." Are we to believe that future centuries will not cast much of what we have established as irrefutable facts into the closet of "blind" superstition? I am certainly convinced that there is real progress in human knowledge. Once the "fact" that the earth is round had been discovered, all earlier suppositions were banished into the realm of "superstition." So it is with certain truths of astronomy, biology, and so on. The doctrine of natural descent, in comparison with all earlier hypotheses of Creation, represents a form of progress that is similar to the idea of a round earth compared to previous assumptions about its shape.

Nevertheless, I am aware that, in our learned scientific works and treatises, there are many so-called facts that will not appear as facts to future centuries any more than much of what was maintained by Agrippa and Paracelsus does today. It is not a question of what they considered to be facts, but of the spirit in which they interpreted those facts. In Agrippa's time, there was little understanding of the "natural magic" that he advocated, which seeks what is natural in nature and what is spiritual only in spirit. People held on to the "supernatural magic" that seeks spirit in the realm of the senses, and which Agrippa fought against. For this reason, Abbot Trithemius of Sponheim advised him to communicate his views as a secret doctrine only to a chosen few, who were able to rise to a similar view of nature and spirit; for "we give oxen only hay, not sugar as we do to songbirds."

Perhaps it is this abbot whom Agrippa has to thank for the right perspective. In his *Steganographia*,[95] Trithemius treats, with the most veiled irony, the way of thinking that confuses nature with spirit. In this book, he seems to speak entirely about supernatural phenomena. One who reads it as it is must conclude that the author is speaking of conjuring spirits, of their flight through the air, and so on. But if one omits certain words and letters in the text, there remain letters that, when assembled into words, describe purely natural phenomena (as Wolfgang Ernst Heidel showed in 1676). (In one case, for example, in a formula of incantation, one must completely omit the first and the last words and then cross out every other word, starting with the second. In the remaining words, one must cross out every other letter, starting with the first. One then assembles what remains into words, and the formula of the incantation is transformed into a communication of a purely natural meaning.)

How difficult it was for Agrippa to work his way out of the prejudices of his time and rise to a clear view is established by the fact that he did not allow his *Occult Philosophy* (*De occulta philosophia*),[96] written in 1510, to be published until 1531, as he considered it premature. Further evidence of his reticence is provided by his work *On the Vanity of the Sciences* (*De vanitate scientiarum*),[97] in which he speaks bitterly of the scientific and general activity of his time. There he says very clearly that only with difficulty did he liberate himself from the delusion of those who see direct spiritual processes in external events, prophetic hints about the future in outer facts, and so on.

Agrippa progresses to higher understanding in three stages. The first stage deals with the world as presented to the senses – with substances and with physical, chemical, and other forces. At this stage, he terms nature *elemental*. The second stage sees the world as a whole in its natural relationships and arrangements of everything related to measurement, number, weight, harmony, and so on. The first stage brings together the attributes that are closely related and looks for the causes of a phenomenon in its immediate environment. The second stage looks at a single phenomenon in relation to the cosmic whole. Agrippa develops the idea that each thing is under the influence of all the remaining things of the cosmic whole. This universal whole appears as a great harmony, of which every individual entity is a part. Seen from this perspective, the world is designated by Agrippa as the astral or heavenly world. The third stage of understanding is where the spirit, through immersion in itself, beholds the spiritual, the primordial essence of the world, directly. Here Agrippa speaks of the "spiritual-soul" world.

The views developed by Agrippa about the world and the human relationship to it are found in a similar, yet more complete form in the work of Theophrastus Paracelsus.

Paracelsus characterized himself when he wrote under his portrait, "No one who can stand alone should be the servant of another." His whole position with regard to knowledge is given in these words. He chose to go back to the foundations of natural science in order to ascend, through his own powers, to the highest regions of understanding. As a physician, he did not want to simply accept, as his contemporaries did, what the old investigators had asserted in the past, although they were considered authorities at the time (Galen or Avicenna, for example). Paracelsus wanted to read directly in the *book of nature*:

> The physician must undergo nature's examination, which is the world and all its beginnings. And what nature teaches him, he must commit to his wisdom; though he must seek nothing in his own wisdom, but only in the light of nature.[98]

He never retreated in his efforts to know nature and its manifestations from every aspect. For this purpose, he traveled to Sweden, Hungary, Spain, Portugal, and the East. He was able to say:

> I have pursued the art despite danger to my life, and I have not been ashamed to learn from vagabonds, executioners, and barbers. My teachings have been tested more severely than silver through poverty, anxiety, wars, and hardships.[99]

Knowledge passed down from old authorities held no value for him; he believed that he could gain the correct view only by experiencing for himself the ascent from natural science to the highest levels of understanding. He boldly articulated his experience:

> One who wants to pursue the truth must come into my realm.[100]
>
> After me, not I after you, Avicenna, Rhases, Galen, Mesur! After me, and not I after you, you of Paris, you of Montpellier, you of Swabia, you of Meissen, you of Cologne, you of Vienna and whatever lies on the Danube and the river Rhine, you islands in the sea, you Italy, you Dalmatia, you Athens, you Greek, you Arab, you Israelite. After me, and not I after you! Mine is the realm![101]

It is easy to misinterpret Paracelsus because of his rough exterior, which sometimes hides his deep seriousness behind jest. As he said of himself:

> Nature did not spin me subtly . . . nor have I been raised on figs and white bread but on cheese,

> milk, and oat bread. Therefore, I may well be uncivil to the excessively clean and overly refined; understanding is difficult between those brought up in soft clothes and those of us who were brought up among pine cones.[102]
>
> Although to myself I appear gracious, I must seem rough to others. How can I not be strange for one who has never gone wandering in the sun?[103]

Goethe has beautifully described the relationship between humankind and nature (in his book on Winckelmann):

> When the healthy nature of the human being works as a whole; when he feels himself in the world as though in a great, beautiful, worthy, and precious whole; when his harmonious sense of well-being imparts to him a pure, free delight; then the universe, if it could experience itself, would, *as having achieved its goal, exult with joy and marvel at the pinnacle of its own becoming and being.*[104]

Paracelsus is deeply permeated with this sentiment. Out of it, the riddle of the human being takes shape for him.

Now let us consider how this happens in Paracelsus's sense. Initially, the road that nature took to bring forth the pinnacle of its becoming is hidden from human powers of comprehension. Nature has attained a pinnacle, but this pinnacle does not say, "I experience myself as the whole of nature," but rather, "I experience myself as an individual human being." What, in fact, is an act of the whole world, comprehends itself as a single, solitary being standing alone. Indeed, this is true human nature: that we must experience ourselves as something other than what we are. And if this is a contradiction, then the human being can be called a contradiction come to life. The human being is the world in his own way. He views his harmony with the world as twofold. He is the same as the world but as a repetition, as an individuated being. This is the contrast that Paracelsus experienced as microcosm (human being) and macrocosm (universe). For him, the human being is the world writ small.

What allows the human being to regard his relationship with the world in this way is his own spirit. This spirit seems bound to a single being, to one organism. In the totality of its being, this organism belongs to the great stream of the universe. It is a part of the whole, existing only in connection with all other beings. Spirit, however, seems to be a result of this single organism. At first, it sees itself as connected only with this organism. It tears the organism from the native soil from which it grew. For Paracelsus, there is a deep connection between the human being and the entire universe – a connection that is hidden in the natural foundation of existence and obscured by the presence of spirit. Spirit leads us to higher understanding by communicating knowledge to us and by bringing that knowledge to rebirth on a higher level. Its initial effect, however, is to mask for us our own connection with the universe.

Paracelsus saw that human nature initially falls into three classifications. The first is our sensory and corporeal nature – the organism that appears to us as a natural being among other natural beings, essentially no different than other natural beings. The second component is our hidden nature. This is a link in the chain of the world in its entirety and is, consequently, not enclosed within our organism. Rather, influences are sent and received between it and the whole universe. The third is our highest nature – our spirit, which only comes to expression spiritually. Paracelsus calls the first part of human nature the *elemental body*; the second he terms the etheric-celestial or *astral body*; and the third part he calls the *soul.* Paracelsus sees "astral" phenomena as an intermediate level, between purely corporeal phenomena and the true soul phenomena. These soul phenomena become visible when the spirit, which veils the natural foundation of our existence, ceases its activity.

We have before us the simplest manifestation of this realm in the dream world. The images that flit through our dreams, with their peculiarly meaningful connections with the events in our environment and with our inner states, are products of our natural foundation that are eclipsed by the soul's brighter light. If a chair collapses near my bed, I may dream a whole drama, ending with the gunshot in a duel. Or my heart may begin to pound and I dream of a red-hot stove. Meaningful and significant natural manifestations appear to reveal a life that exists between purely organic functions and the thinking processes unfolding in the spirit's bright consciousness. All the phenomena of hypnotism and suggestion are related to this. In suggestion, we can see the effect of one human being upon another, which points to an interconnection among natural beings that is veiled by the higher activity of spirit.

Thus it becomes possible to understand what Paracelsus describes as an "astral" body. It is the collection of natural influences to which we are exposed, or to which we can be exposed through special circumstances, as well as those influences which emanate from us without the involvement of our soul, and which do not fall into the category of purely physical phenomena. That Paracelsus enumerates facts in this realm that we would doubt today is no matter of concern for us when seen from the point of view I mentioned above (see pp. 114–15).

Based on such views of the nature of the human being, Paracelsus divides human nature into seven aspects. These aspects are the same as those we find in the teachings of the ancient Egyptians, the Neoplatonists, and the Cabala. Human beings are first of all physical, bodily beings, subject to the same laws to which *any* body is subject. In this sense, the human being is a purely *elemental* body. Purely corporeal, physical laws arrange themselves in the processes of *organic* life. Paracelsus designates the organic laws

Archaeus, or Spiritus Vitae; the organic raises itself to spirit-like manifestations that are not yet spirit. These are the "*astral*" manifestations. Out of the "astral" processes emerge the functions of the "*animal spirit*."

The human being is a sensory being. He brings together sensory impressions through his intellect. Thus the "*intellectual* or *rational soul*" awakens in him. He immerses himself in the results of his own spiritual activity; he learns to recognize the spirit as spirit. In this way, he raises himself to the level of the "*spiritual soul*." Finally, he understands that, in this spiritual soul, he experiences the deepest foundations of universal existence; the spiritual soul ceases to be individual and separate. This is the insight of which Eckhart spoke when he said he felt that it was no longer *he* who spoke, but the primordial presence that spoke within him. The state is reached in which universal spirit beholds itself in the human being. Paracelsus expressed in simple words the feeling aroused by the experience of this state: "And this is something great, which you should ponder: there is nothing in heaven or earth that is not also in the human being. And *God*, who is in heaven – He is in the human being."[105]

What Paracelsus intends to bring to expression through his differentiation of the seven aspects of human nature is nothing other than the facts of outer and inner experience.

It remains undisputed that what appears for

human experience as this plurality of seven parts is, in higher reality, a unity. Higher cognition exists precisely to show the unity in everything that, to immediate experience, appears as a plurality due to our bodily and spiritual organization. At the highest level of understanding, Paracelsus strives to fuse the world's living, uniform, primordial essence with his own spirit. He knows, however, that we can know nature spiritually only when we enter immediate communion with it. We do not come to understand nature by populating it with arbitrarily assumed spiritual entities but by accepting and valuing it as nature. Paracelsus, therefore, does not look for God or spirit *in* nature; for him nature, as it presents itself to his eye, is *divine.* Or must one first attribute to the plant a soul resembling the human soul in order to find spirit? This is why Paracelsus explains the development of phenomena (to the degree that this is possible with the scientific resources of his time) in a manner that places this development entirely within the reaches of natural, sense-perceptible processes. He lets everything arise from primordial matter, primordial water (*Yliaster*). And he regards as a further process of nature the separation of primordial matter (which he also calls the "great limbo") into the four elements of water, earth, fire, and air. When he says that the "divine Word" invoked the multiplicity of beings from primordial matter, this should be understood in somewhat the same way as contemporary natural science understands the relationship between force and matter. A "spirit" in the factual sense is not yet present on this level. This "spirit" is not the actual basis of the natural process but a *result* of this process. This spirit does not create nature but develops from it. Much of what Paracelsus says, however, could be interpreted in the opposite sense. For example, he says:

> There is nothing corporeal that does not carry a living spirit hidden within it. *All* corporeal and substantial things have this life, not just those that stir and move, such as people and animals, the worms in the earth, the birds in the sky, and the fish in the water.[106]

Paracelsus uses such sayings only to warn against a superficial view of nature in which one can exhaust the nature of a phenomenon with a few "forced" concepts (to use Goethe's apt expression). He does not want to project a contrived beingness into things, but to move the human capacity to draw out what actually lives within them. It is important not to be misled by the fact that Paracelsus expresses himself in the spirit of his time. Instead, one should try to understand what he has in mind when, viewing nature, he presents his ideas in the expressions of his time. For example, he ascribes to the human being a twofold flesh – that is, a twofold corporeal constitution.

> The flesh must be understood to be of two kinds – the flesh whose origin is in Adam and the flesh that is not from Adam. The flesh from

> Adam is coarse flesh, because it is earthly and only flesh, to be bound and grasped like wood and stone. The other flesh is not from Adam; it is subtle flesh, not to be bound or grasped, because it is not made of earth.[107]

What is the flesh that comes from Adam? It is all that has come down to us through *natural* evolution, which we have thus *inherited.* Added to this is all that we have *acquired* in the course of time through interacting with our environment. Our contemporary scientific concepts of *inherited* characteristics and those *acquired through adaptation* broke loose from the above-described thoughts of Paracelsus. The "subtler flesh," which makes us capable of spiritual activities, had not been present from the beginning in human beings, who were of "coarse flesh," like the animals, a flesh that can be "bound and grasped like wood and stone." Consequently, in the scientific sense, the soul is also an *acquired* characteristic of this coarse flesh. When scientists of the nineteenth century speak of the inheritances from the animal world, they mean what Paracelsus meant by his expression, the "flesh that came from Adam."

These remarks, of course, are not intended to eliminate the difference between a natural scientist of the sixteenth century and those of the nineteenth century. After all, it was only in the nineteenth century that we gained the ability to see, in a fully scientific sense, the forms of living organisms – including the human being – such that their natural relationships and true derivation became evident. Science sees only a natural process, whereas Linnaeus, in the eighteenth century, still saw a spiritual process, which he characterized in this way: "There are as many species of living organisms as there are, in principle, forms that have been *created*."[108] Whereas Linnaeus had to shift spirit into the spatial world and assign it the task of spiritually producing, or "creating," life-forms, the natural scientist of the nineteenth century could attribute to nature what belongs to nature and to spirit what belongs to spirit. Nature itself is given the task of explaining its creations, and spirit can immerse itself in itself, where it alone may be found – in the inner life of the human being.

But even if Paracelsus, in a certain sense, thinks very much in the spirit of his time, it is nevertheless true that precisely with regard to the idea of *evolution*, or *becoming*, he comprehended the relationship between the human being and nature in a profound way. He did not see the world's primordial essence as something finished; he grasped instead the Divine in its process of becoming. Consequently, he could in truth ascribe self-creating activity to the human being. If the divine, primordial essence were present in its completeness, then true creation by the human being is out of the question. Then it could not be the human being, living in time, who creates, but God, who is eternal. For Paracelsus, there is no eternal God. For him there is only eternal becoming, and the human being is a link in this eternal becoming. What the human being forms did not exist previously in any way. Whatever the human being creates is an original creation. If it is to be called divine, then it can be called so only in the sense that it exists as a human creation. Accordingly, in terms of cosmic creation, Paracelsus can assign to the human being a role that makes him into co-architect of this creation.

Without the human being, the divine, primordial essence is not the same as what it is *with* the human being. "For nature brings forth nothing into the light of day complete as it stands; rather, the human being must complete it."[109] The self-creating activity of the human being in the formation of nature, Paracelsus calls *alchemy.* "This completion is alchemy. Alchemists are bakers when they bake bread, vintners when they make wine, weavers when they make cloth."[110] Paracelsus desires to be an alchemist in his field, as a physician.

> I may fittingly write so much here about alchemy that you learn it well and know what it is and how it is to be understood; do not be annoyed that it is not intended to bring you gold or silver. Rather, contemplate it so that the arcana (the means of healing) are revealed to you.[111]
>
> The third pillar of medicine is alchemy, for the preparation of remedies cannot take place without it, *because nature cannot be put to use without art.*[112]

Paracelsus's eyes are directed, in the strictest sense, at nature, in order to discover from nature itself what it says about what it brings forth. He investigates the laws of chemistry so that he can work in this sense as an alchemist. He imagines all bodies to be composed of three basic substances – salt, sulfur, and mercury. These do not, of course, correspond with the terminology of modern chemistry, nor does what Paracelsus considers to be basic substance. The same names designate different things at different times. The ancients designated phenomena according to the four elements – earth, water, air, and fire – and these are still with us. We no longer call them "elements" but states of aggregation, which we term solid, liquid, gaseous, and ethereal. For example, for the ancients *earth* did not refer to the earth but to "solidity." We can also recognize the three basic substances of Paracelsus in contemporary concepts, although not in the words he used. For Paracelsus, "solution in a liquid" and "combustion" were the two important chemical processes that he employed. When a body is dissolved or burned, it disintegrates into its parts. Something remains as residue, and something is dissolved or burned. He saw the residue as saline, the soluble (fluid) as mercurial, and the combustible as sulfurous.

To one who fails to look beyond such natural processes, these processes may appear merely material and prosaic, leaving him cold. One who wishes at all costs to apprehend spirit through the senses will populate these processes with all sorts of soul beings. Like Paracelsus, however, one who knows how to view such processes in relation to the universe – which reveals its secrets within the human being – accepts these processes as they are perceived by the senses. One does not begin by reinterpreting them; for these natural processes, as they appear before us in their sensory reality, reveal in their own way the riddle of existence. What these natural processes, through their sensory reality, are able to reveal from out of the human soul, stands – for one who strives toward the light of higher cognition – higher than any supernatural wonders that the human being could devise, or have revealed to him, concerning the supposed "spirit" of these natural processes. There is no "spirit of nature" that can express any truths higher than those revealed by the great works of nature itself, when our soul unites with nature in friendship, and, in intimate exchange, heeds the revelations of its secrets. Paracelsus sought this quality of friendship with nature.

.V.

VALENTIN WEIGEL AND JACOB BOEHME

Paracelsus was concerned primarily with developing ideas about nature that breathed the spirit of higher understanding he advocated. Valentin Weigel (1533–1588) was a kindred thinker. He applied the same kind of thinking to human nature. His thinking grew out of Protestant theology, just as Eckhart's, Tauler's, and Suso's grew out of Catholic theology. He followed in the footsteps of Sebastian Franck and Caspar Schwenckfeldt. They emphasized the deepening of the inner life, in contrast to the Church's attachment to an external creed. For them, it is not the Jesus about whom the Gospels preach who is of value, but rather the Christ, who can be born in every human being out of one's deeper nature as the deliverer from the lower aspects of life and the guide in the ascent toward the ideal. Weigel lived quietly and modestly as pastor of his church in Zschopau. His writings were printed posthumously in the seventeenth century. From them, one discovers the significant ideas he developed concerning human nature. (Three of Weigel's works are: *The Golden Grasp for Discerning All Things without Error, Unknown to All the Universities, yet Necessary for All Human Beings to Know*; *Know Thyself*; and *On the Place of the World*.)[113]

Weigel was anxious to gain clarity concerning his relationship to the Church's teachings, and was consequently led to investigate the fundaments of cognition in general. It is only possible to ascertain whether a creed provides a basis for knowledge if we first understand *how* we come to know. Weigel began with the most basic kind of cognition. He asked: How do I apprehend a sensory object that I encounter? From there he hoped to rise to the point where he could account for the highest form of cognition. In sensory apprehension, the instrument (the sensory organ) and the object, the "counterpart," stand across from each other:

> In natural perception, there must be two things: the object or counterpart that is to be known and seen by the eye; and the eye, or perceiver, which sees and knows the object. Therefore, consider this question: Does knowledge arise from the object and flow into the eye, or do judgment and knowledge flow from the eye into the object? (*The Golden Grasp*, chapter 9)

Weigel ponders that if knowledge flowed from the counterpart (the object) into the eye, then the same complete knowledge would have to arise in all eyes with respect to the same object. But this is not so; we all see according to our own eyes. Only the eyes, not the counterpart, can be responsible for the fact that many different views of one and the same thing are possible. In order to make the matter clear, Weigel compares seeing with reading. If the book did not exist, then I could not read it. But it could be there, and I would still not be able to read anything in it if I did not know how to read. The book is there, but cannot itself give me anything; I must evoke within myself everything I read. This is also true of natural (sensory) knowledge. Color exists as a "counterpart" but, of itself, cannot offer anything to the eye. The eye itself must come to know color. The color is no more in the eye than the content of the book is in the reader. If the content of the book were in us as readers, we would not have to read it. Nevertheless, in reading, this content does not flow out of the book but out of the reader. It is the same with sensory objects. The nature of the sensory object out there does not flow into the human being from the outside but from the inside.

Based on these ideas, one could say that if all knowledge flows from the human being into the object, one does not know what is in the object but only what is within the human being. The views of Immanuel Kant (1724–1804) present a detailed elaboration of this line of thinking. (I have shown the erroneous aspect of this train of thought in chapter IV of my book *The Philosophy of Spiritual Activity*. Here I must limit myself to saying that with his simple, natural way of thinking, Valentin Weigel stands on a much higher level than does Kant.) Weigel says to himself: Even though knowledge flows from the human being, it is indeed still only the essence of the counterpart that comes to expression through this detour of the human observer. Just as it is the content of the book that I discover by reading, and not my own content, so it is the color of the counterpart that I discover through the eye, not any color that is in the eye itself or in me. Following his own path, Weigel thus concludes what we have already encountered in the thinking of Nicholas of Cusa.

Weigel clarified for himself the nature of sensory knowledge. He became convinced that whatever external objects have to say to us can flow only from within our own inner self. When the human being wants to know the things of the sense world, he cannot remain passive and want to merely let things work upon him; rather, he must become active and bring this knowledge out of *himself*. The counterpart awakens knowledge only in the spirit. The human being ascends to higher cognition when the spirit becomes its own object.

In coming to an understanding of the nature of sensory knowledge, one recognizes that no knowledge can flow into the human being from outside. Accordingly, higher knowledge also cannot come from outside but must be awakened within the human being. There can be no external revelation, but only an inner awakening. Just as an external object must wait until the human being, within whom it can express its nature, encounters it, so must the human being wishing to become his own counterpart also wait until knowledge of his own nature is awakened within him. Whereas in sensory knowledge, it is necessary for the human being to become active in order that he may bring forth for the counterpart its nature, in higher knowledge, he must remain passive, because he is now counterpart *himself*. He must receive his own inner nature from within. Consequently, spiritual knowledge appears as higher illumination.

Weigel therefore calls higher knowledge, as opposed to sensory or natural knowledge, the "light of grace." This "light of grace" is in fact nothing other than the self-knowledge of the human spirit – a rebirth of knowledge on a higher level of seeing. In pursuing his path from knowing to seeing, Nicholas of Cusa does not really allow the knowledge he acquires to be reborn on a higher level; rather, the religious confession in which he was educated appears deceptively as this rebirth. This is the case with Weigel also. He finds the right path and loses it again as soon as he begins to follow it. If we want to follow the way indicated by Weigel, we can look to him as our guide only to where the path begins.

* * *

In the works of Jacob Boehme (1575–1624), the master shoemaker of Görlitz, we can almost hear nature singing with joy when, having reached its highest point, it gazes with wonder upon its own being. Here is a man whose words have wings woven from the blissful feeling that comes with seeing the knowledge he bears within shining as higher wisdom. Boehme describes his condition as devotion that desires only to be wisdom, as wisdom that desires only to live in devotion:

> When, in God's supportive presence, I wrestled and fought, a wondrous light arose within my soul that was completely foreign to wild nature. Through it, I recognized for the first time what God and the human being are, and what God has to do with humankind.[114]

Jacob Boehme no longer experienced himself as a separate personality expressing his personal insights; he experienced himself as an organ of the great universal spirit who spoke within him. The limits of his personality did not appear to him to be limits of the spirit speaking out of him. This spirit is omnipresent for him. He knows that "the sophist wants to rebuke him" whenever he speaks of the world's beginning and creation,

> because I was not there and did not see it myself. Let them be told that, when I was not yet the 'I' but still Adam's essence, in the essence of my soul and body I was indeed there, and that I have sacrificed my glory in Adam.[115]

Only in outer parables can Boehme suggest the nature of the light that shined within him. Once, as a boy, he found himself at the top of a mountain. Amidst great red stones that appeared to cap the peak, he saw an entrance open. In its depths, he beheld a vessel of gold. He was overcome with awe and went on his way without touching the treasure. Later, when he was an apprentice with a shoemaker in Görlitz, a stranger walked into the store and asked for a pair of shoes. Boehme was not allowed to sell them to him in the master's absence. The stranger left, but after a while, he called the apprentice outside and said, "Jacob, you are young, but one day you will become a completely different person who will astonish the whole world."

Older and more mature, Jacob Boehme once saw the sun reflected in a burnished, pewter vessel; the sight that confronted him seemed to reveal a profound mystery. After his experience of that manifestation, he believed he possessed the key to the mysterious language of nature. He lived as a spiritual hermit and supported himself modestly by his trade. He wrote down, as if for his own memory, the notes that sounded within when he felt the spirit in him. The fanatic zeal of the priests made his life difficult. He wanted to read only the scriptures that illuminated the light that shone within him, but he was pursued and tormented by those who had access only to the external scriptures of rigid, dogmatic religious belief.

A world-riddle lived in Boehme's soul. It left him restless and drove him to seek knowledge. He believed that he was immersed with his spirit in a divine harmony; but when he looked around, he saw disharmony everywhere in the divine works. The human being can receive the light of wisdom – and still, he is exposed to error. The impulse toward good lives in people, yet the dissonance of evil can be heard throughout the course of human evolution. Nature is governed by grand laws, yet its harmony is disturbed by excesses and the wild struggle of the elements.

How is this disharmony to be understood within the harmonious, universal whole?

This question tormented Boehme. It became the focus of his world of ideas. He aspired to achieve a concept of the universal whole that includes the disharmonious. For how can a worldview clarify the world if it leaves this existing disharmony unexplained?

Disharmony must be understood as deriving from harmony, and evil must be understood as deriving from good. In discussing these matters, let us limit ourselves to forms of good and evil in which disharmony in the narrower sense finds its expression in human life. For fundamentally, Jacob Boehme limits himself to that. He can, for to him, nature and the human being appear as one being. He sees in both similar laws and processes. To him, inexpediency is nature's evil, just as evil, to him, is human destiny's inexpedience. The same basic forces hold sway in both. To one who understands the origin of evil in the human being, the origin of evil in nature is also evident.

How can it be that evil as well as good flow from the same original being [*Urwesen*]? If we approach this question as Boehme did, we would answer it as follows: Original being does not live out its existence in isolation. The manifoldness of the world participates in its existence. Just as the human being exists not as a single entity but as a multiplicity of members, so likewise does original being. And just as a human life is poured out into this multiplicity of members, so original being is poured out into the manifoldness of the world. It is just as true that the whole human being has *a single* life, as it is that each member has a life of its own. And as little as it contradicts the complete harmony of human life for the hand to turn against its own body and do it harm, just as little would it be impossible for the things of the world, each of which lives the life of the original being in its own way, to turn against one another. Thus, by splitting itself up into different lives, original life bestows upon each single life the capacity to turn against the whole. It is not from the Good that the Evil emanates, but from the manner in which the Good exists. As light can only shine when it intermingles with the darkness, so the Good can only bring itself to life when it permeates its opposite. From out of the "un-ground" [*Ungrund*] of darkness, the light begins to shine; from out of the "un-ground" of indifference, the Good gives birth to itself. And just as, in the case of shadow, it is only the brightness that prompts us to ask after the light, while it goes without saying that the darkness weakens the light: so likewise, in the world, it is only lawfulness that is sought for in all things, whereas evil – that which is inexpedient – is taken for granted. Despite the fact that, for Jacob Boehme, original being is the all-in-all, it is nevertheless true that, for him, nothing in the world can be understood if one does not have in view both original being and its opposite.

> The Good has absorbed the Evil or the abominable into itself. . . . Every being has good and evil within itself; and in its unfolding, insofar as this leads it into a state of divergence, there emerges an opposition [*Contrarium*] of qualities in which one seeks to overcome the other.[116]

Thus it is entirely in the spirit of Jacob Boehme to see both good and evil in the world's every object and process, but it is not in his spirit to seek original being without further ado in the mixture of good and evil. Original being had to assimilate evil, but evil is not a part of original being. Boehme sought the original ground of being [*Urgrund*] of the world; the world, however, was itself raised from the un-ground by the original ground.

> The external world is not God, and for all eternity shall not be called God; but it is only a being in which God reveals Himself.[117]
>
> When one says "God is everything – God is heaven and earth and also the outer world," this is indeed true; for everything originates from Him and in Him. But what am I to do with such a saying that is not religion?[118]

With this view as a background, Boehme's ideas about the nature of the world developed in his spirit so that he saw the lawful world as arising out of the un-ground in a succession of stages. This world is built up in seven natural forms.

Original being takes on form as a dark bitterness, silently enclosed within itself and motionless. Boehme apprehends this bitterness through the symbol of Salt. In doing so, he follows in the footsteps of Paracelsus, who borrowed terms for natural processes from chemical processes (see p. 130 above). By incorporating its opposite, the first natural form assumes the shape of the second. Bitter inertness embodies mobility – energy and life enter it. Mercury symbolizes the second natural form. In the struggle between stillness and motion, between death and life, the third natural form (Sulfur) appears. Life, with its inner conflict, is revealed to itself; it no longer lives in the external struggle of its parts; like uniformly shining lightning illuminating itself, it delights in its own being (Fire).

The fourth natural form then ascends to the fifth – the living struggle of the parts, which rests within itself (Water). On this level, there is an inner bitterness and silence that is similar to the first. It is not an absolute quiet of inner contrasts, but an inner movement of contrasts. It is not quiet that rests within itself, but motion that was kindled by the fiery lightning of the fourth stage. On the sixth level, original being becomes aware of its inner life; it perceives itself through the sensory organs. Living organisms, endowed with senses, bring this natural form to expression. Boehme calls it Sound, or resonance, and thus establishes the sensation of hearing as the symbol of sensory perception in general. The seventh natural form is the spirit elevating itself on the basis of its sensory perceptions (Wisdom). It finds itself once again – within the world that has grown out of the un-ground and formed itself from the harmonic and dissonant – as itself, as the original ground of being. "The Holy Spirit leads the splendor of majesty into the entity in which the Divinity is revealed."[119]

On the basis of such ideas, Jacob Boehme sought to fathom *that* world which, in keeping with the knowledge of his time, he held to be real. For him, the "facts" were established by the natural science of his time and by the Bible. His way of thinking is one thing and his world of facts another. One can imagine his way of thinking applied to a very different set of facts. Accordingly, we see before us a Boehme who could be living at the beginning of the twentieth century. Such a man would not use his thinking to understand the biblical story of Creation and the struggle between the angels and devils; rather, he would use Lyell's *Principles of Geography* and Haeckel's *Natural History of Creation*.[120] One who gets through to an understanding of the *spirit* of Boehme's writings must arrive at this conviction. (The most important of these writings are: *The Coming of the Dawn*; *Concerning the Three Principles of the Divine Essence*; *The Threefold Life of Man*; *The Eye Turned upon Itself*; *Signatura Rerum or the Signature of All Things*; and *Mysterium Magnum*.)[121, d]

[d] See addendum IV, p. 172.

.VI.

GIORDANO BRUNO AND ANGELUS SILESIUS

At Castle Heilsberg in Prussia, during the first decade of the sixteenth century, the scientific genius Nicolaus Copernicus (1473–1543) erected a framework of ideas that compelled those of following eras to gaze at the starry heavens in a way unlike that of our predecessors of antiquity or the Middle Ages. To the people of medieval times, the earth was a dwelling at rest in the center of the universe. The stars, on the other hand, were perfect beings that moved in circles, the circle representing the image of perfection. Human beings saw in the sensory manifestations of the stars something belonging directly to the soul or the spirit. The objects and events of the earth spoke one language to humankind; another language was spoken by the shining stars, which, in the pure ether beyond the moon, appeared as spiritual beings filling all of space. Nicholas of Cusa had already formed different ideas. Through the explanations of Copernicus, the earth became for humankind a creation among other heavenly bodies, a star that moved like the others. Any differences in humanity's conception of the earth could only be attributed to the fact that we live here. People were forced to stop viewing earthly phenomena any differently than they did the rest of the universe. The sensory world had expanded into the most distant reaches of space. They had to accept that everything that reaches the eye from the ether is a part of the sensory realm, no different than the things of the earth. They could no longer look for spirit in the sense-experienced ether.

All who strove for higher knowledge had to come to terms with this expanded sensory world. In earlier centuries, the contemplative human spirit had faced a different world. Now it was given a new task. No longer was it only the things of the earth that could express their nature from within the human being. This living inner space had to embrace the spirit of a sensory world that permeates the entire spatial universe in the same way. This was the kind of task that confronted Philotheo Giordano Bruno (1548–1600), the thinker from Nola.

The senses had conquered the spatial universe for themselves; spirit could no longer be found in space. Consequently, human beings were prompted from without to look for spirit only where it had been sought on the basis of deep inner experiences by the superb thinkers I have discussed in the preceding chapters. These thinkers drew out of themselves a worldview that advances in natural science would later force upon humankind. The sun of ideas that later illuminated a new understanding of nature was still beyond the horizon for those thinkers, but even then its light appeared as an approaching dawn when human thinking about nature was still enclosed within the darkness of night.

For the purposes of science, the sixteenth century gave the heavens to the world of the senses, to which they rightfully belong. By the end of the nineteenth century, science had progressed to the degree that it could attribute to the sensory world the phenomena of plant, animal, and human life that rightfully belonged to it. Neither in the ether nor in the development of living organisms could science henceforth look for anything other than processes based on sense-perceptible facts. The sixteenth-century thinker was compelled to say that the earth is a star among stars, subject to the same laws as other stars. And the nineteenth-century thinker had to say:

> Whatever their origin and future may be, in the context of anthropology human beings are only mammals. Specifically, they are mammals whose organization, needs, and diseases are the most complicated and whose brain, with its wonderful capacity, has reached the highest degree of development. (Paul Topinard, *Anthropology*)[122]

Based on this scientifically-acquired perspective, it has become impossible to confuse the spirit and the sensory world as long as people understand themselves correctly. Advanced science makes it impossible to search for an embodied spirit in nature, just as sound thinking compels us to look at the laws of mechanics (the spirit of inorganic nature) to find out why the hands of a clock advance rather than looking for a particular demon that causes the hands to move. As a scientist, Ernst Haeckel justifiably rejected the clumsy view of a material god:

> In the higher, more abstract forms of religion, this corporeal manifestation is abandoned, and God is worshiped only as "*pure spirit*," without a body. "God is a Spirit: and they that worship Him must worship Him in spirit and in truth."[123] Nevertheless, the spiritual activity of this pure spirit is exactly the same as that of the anthropomorphous, divine personality. In reality, this immaterial spirit, too, is not thought of as incorporeal but as invisible, gaseous. We thus come to the paradoxical view of God as a *gas-like vertebrate*.[124]

In fact, the actual sensory existence of a spiritual reality can be assumed only where an immediate sensory experience reveals the spirit; and spirit can be presupposed only to the degree that it is perceived in this way. The great thinker B. Carneri said (in the book *Sensation and Consciousness*):[125]

> The words "no spirit without matter, but also no matter without spirit" would justify extending the problem to plants or even to the first rock we encounter, in which hardly anything could be said in favor of this correlation.

Spiritual processes, as actualities, are the results of various functions of an organism; the spirit of the world does not exist in the world in a material way, but in a spiritual way only. The human soul is the sum of the processes in which spirit appears most directly *as an actuality*. But it is *only* in the human being that spirit is ensouled in this way. To look for spirit in the form of a soul anywhere other than in the human being – to view other beings as endowed with a soul like that of a human being – is to misunderstand spirit; it is to commit the most grievous sin against the spirit. Whoever does so shows that he has not experienced the actual spirit within himself, but only what holds sway in him as the external manifestation of the spirit – namely, the soul. It is as if someone were to mistake a circle drawn in pencil for the true mathematical ideal circle. Whoever experiences within himself nothing other than the *soul-form* of spirit, feels the need to assume such a soul-form in nonhuman things so that he does not have to stop at coarse sensory materiality. Instead of conceiving of the primordial foundation of the world as spirit, he thinks of it as a world soul and assumes a general ensoulment of nature.

Under the impact of the new Copernican view of nature, Giordano Bruno could grasp the spirit in the world – out of which it had been driven in its old form – only as a *world soul*. Those who immerse themselves in Bruno's writings (especially his profound book *Cause, Principle and Unity*),[126] have the impression that he conceived of things as ensouled, though to various degrees. He had not experienced true spirit within himself, and thus imagined spirit in terms of the human soul – in the only form in which he had encountered it. When he speaks of the spirit, he understands it in this way. "Universal reason is the most inward, real, and characteristic faculty, and it is a potential part of the world soul; it is the same everywhere and fills the all-in-all; it illuminates the universe and instructs nature in producing its species as they should be."[127] Here the spirit is not described as a "gas-like vertebrate," but as a being like the human soul. "A thing, however minute, has within itself a portion of spiritual substance that, if it finds the substratum to be suitable, strives to become a plant or an animal and organizes itself into some kind of body, which is generally considered ensouled. Spirit may be found in all things, and there is not the most minute body that does not contain such a portion of it that it animates itself."[128]

Because Giordano Bruno had not really experienced spirit as such within himself, he could confuse the life of spirit with those outer mechanical functions by means of which Ramon Llull (1235–1315), in his so-called "Great Art," had attempted to unveil the mysteries of the spirit. The modern philosopher Franz Brentano described the "Great Art": "Various concepts were inscribed on concentric, circular disks that can be turned individually, and in this way, diverse combinations were produced."[129] What coincidence caused to be superimposed on a particular turn was formed into a judgment concerning the highest truths. During his extensive wanderings throughout Europe, Giordano Bruno appeared at various universities as a teacher of the "Great Art." He was bold enough to conceive of the stars as worlds completely analogous to our earth. He enlarged the vision of scientific thinking beyond the earth; he no longer thought of the *heavenly bodies* as *corporeal* spirits but he did still conceive of them as being *ensouled* spirits. One must not do an injustice to this man whom the Catholic Church put to death for his advanced ideas. It was an enormous achievement to enfold the entire heavenly expanse within the same concept of the world that until then had been applied only to earthly things, even if Bruno envisioned the sensory realm as being soul-like.

* * *

In the seventeenth century, the thinker Johannes Scheffler, known as Angelus Silesius (1624–1677), let the visions of Tauler, Weigel, Jacob Boehme, and others shine forth once more in great spiritual harmony. Their ideas appear in his book *Cherubinic Wanderer* as though newly focused and radiating a heightened luminosity. Everything Silesius said appears as such a direct and spontaneous revelation of his personality that it seems as though he was destined by providence to embody wisdom in a personal form. The natural way his life expressed that wisdom is shown in his sayings, which may likewise be admired for their artistic quality. He hovered above earthly existence like a spiritual being, and what he said is like a breath from another world, cleansed entirely of all those coarse and impure elements that human wisdom must struggle to leave behind.

According to the outlook of Angelus Silesius, only those who cause the eye of the All to see within them may partake of true cognition, and only those who feel that their actions are performed by the hand of the All may see these actions in their true light:

> God is the fire within me, and I am the light in Him. Are we not quite intimately connected to each other?
>
> I am as rich as God; there can be no grain of dust – dear people, believe me – that I do not have in common with Him.
>
> God loves me above Himself. If I love Him above myself, then I give Him as much as He gives to me out of Himself.
>
> The bird flies in the air, the stone lies on the land; in the water lives the fish, and my spirit in God's hand.
>
> If you are born of God, then God blossoms in you: and His divinity is your sap and adornment.
>
> Stop – where are you running to? Heaven is within you. If you seek God anywhere else, you will miss Him time and time again.[130]

For one who feels that he exists in the All in this way, all separation between himself and other beings ceases. He no longer views himself as a separate individual; rather, he feels that everything about him is a part of the world and that his true essence is identical with the universe itself.

> The world does not hold you back. Rather, you are the world that, within you and with you, keeps you so strongly imprisoned.
>
> The human being will not have perfect blessedness until oneness has swallowed the otherness.
>
> The human being is all things; if he lacks something, then he himself truly does not know his own wealth.[131]

As a sensory being, the human being is a "thing" among other things, and his sensory organs give him, as a sensing individuality, information about the objects outside himself in space and time. However, when spirit speaks in the human being, "outside" and "inside" cease to exist. Nothing spiritual is here or there, earlier or later. Space and time disappear in contemplating universal spirit. Only as long as the human being sees as an individual is he "here" and the thing "there"; and only as long as he sees as an individual is one thing earlier and another later:

> Friends, when you let your spirit rise above place and time, you can be in eternity at every moment.
>
> I myself am eternity when I leave time and collect myself in God, and God in myself.
>
> The rose that your outer eye here sees – it has, from eternity, blossomed like this in God.
>
> Sit in the center, and you will see everything

> at once: what happens both now and then, both here and in heaven.
>
> As long, my friend, as place and time are in your mind, you will not comprehend what God is and what eternity.
>
> When the human being withdraws from multiplicity and returns himself to God, he comes to unity.[132]

With this, the height has been scaled at which the human being goes beyond his individual 'I' and abolishes every distinction between world and self. A higher life begins for him. The inner experience that comes over him appears to him as the death of the old and a resurrection in new life.

> When you rise above yourself and let God hold sway: then, in your spirit, the Ascension will be held.
>
> The body must elevate itself in the spirit, and the spirit in God: if you, dear friend, wish to live in Him in eternal blessedness.
>
> As much as my 'I' pines away and diminishes in me: so much is the 'I' of the Lord strengthened.[133]

From this point of view, the human being recognizes his significance and that of everything else in the realm of eternal necessity. The natural universe appears to him at once as the divine spirit. The thought of a divine, universal spirit that could have its being and duration above and alongside the things of the world fades away as an idea that has been overcome.

This universal spirit seems to have flowed out

so completely into things, seems to have become so entirely one with the nature of things – that it is no longer possible to conceive of it if even a single member is subtracted from its being in thought. "There is nothing but I and you; and if we two do not exist, then God is God no more, and the heavens will collapse."[134] The human being feels himself to be a necessary link in the chain of the world. His actions no longer have any element of arbitrariness or individuality. What he does is necessary for the whole, for the world chain, which would fall apart if these actions were to be taken out of it.

> Without me, God cannot make a single worm: if I do not preserve it with Him, it must straightaway fall to pieces.
>
> I know that without me God cannot live for an instant: if I come to nothing, He must of necessity give up the ghost.[135]

Only from this height does one first see things as they truly are. One no longer needs to append, from outside, a spiritual essence to the smallest, coarsest phenomenon. For this smallest of things is – in all its smallness and its coarse-sensory nature – a member of the All.

> No speck of dust is so poor, no dot so small: the wise one sees God in His glory therein.
>
> In a mustard seed, if you will understand it, is the image of all higher and lower things.[136]

At this height, one feels oneself free. For, coercion exists only where something can compel one from outside. When all externality has flowed into the interior, when the contrast between "I and world," "outside and inside," "nature and spirit" has disappeared – then, all that drives one is felt to be solely an expression of one's own impulse.

> Bind me as tight as you like, in a thousand irons: I will nevertheless be completely free and unfettered.
>
> Insofar as *my* will is dead, then God *must* do what I will: I myself prescribe for Him the pattern and the goal.[137]

Now all externally imposed moral norms cease; the human being becomes his own measure and goal. He is not subject to any law, because the law, too, has become *his* own nature. "The law is for the wicked; if no commandment were written, the godly would nevertheless love God and their neighbors."[138] On the higher level of cognition, the *innocence of nature* is returned to the human being. He accomplishes the tasks assigned to him with the feeling of an eternal necessity. He says to himself: Through this iron necessity, you are given the possibility of withdrawing from this same eternal necessity the member that has been apportioned to you.

> Dear people, learn from the little flower of the meadow: how you can please God and be beautiful at the same time.
>
> The rose does not ask why; it blooms because it blooms. It pays no attention to itself and does not wonder if anyone sees it.[139]

The person who rises to a higher level of understanding feels within himself the eternal and necessary impulse of the universe, just like the flower of the meadow; he acts in the same way as the flower of the meadow blooms. In all his actions, the feeling of his moral responsibility grows immeasurably. For what he fails to do is withdrawn from the All-Being; it kills this All-Being, insofar as it is possible for him to do so.

> What does it mean not to sin? You may not ask for long: go, the silent flowers will tell you.
>
> Everything must be slain. If you do not slay yourself for God, then in the end, eternal death will slay you for the enemy.[140]

EPILOGUE

Almost two and a half centuries have passed since Angelus Silesius gathered in *Cherubinic Wanderer* the profound wisdom of his precursors. Those centuries have brought rich insights into nature. Goethe opened a vast perspective in natural science. He pursued the eternally fixed laws of nature's work up to the ultimate height where they produced humankind just as inevitably as, on a lower level, they produce stones (see my book *Goethe's Worldview*).[141] Lamarck, Darwin, Haeckel, and others continued to work in the spirit of this way of thinking.

The "question of questions," concerning the natural origins of humanity, was answered in the nineteenth century. Other related questions concerning processes in the realm of nature have also been solved. Today we know that it is unnecessary to go beyond the realm of facts and the senses to understand, in a purely natural way, the evolutionary sequence of beings up to the human being. The nature of the human 'I,' too, has been illuminated by the intellectual brilliance of J. G. Fichte, who described the human soul in a manner that showed it where to look for itself (see pp. 20–21 above and the sections on Fichte in my book *Riddles of Philosophy*). Hegel extended the domain of thought to cover all fields of being and endeavored to comprehend in thought the outer, sensory existence of nature, as well as the highest creations of the human spirit and the laws that govern them (see my presentation of Hegel in *Riddles of Philosophy*).

How do the individualities whose thinking this work outlines appear in the light of a worldview that includes the scientific advancements of periods since theirs? They still believed in a "supernatural" history of Creation. How do their thoughts appear in the face of "natural" views developed by nineteenth-century science? Science has not attributed anything to nature that does not belong there; it has removed from nature only what does not belong to it. Science rid nature of everything that cannot be found there but is only to be found within the human being. Science no longer sees a force in nature that resembles the human soul and creates in the manner of a human being. It no longer provides for the idea that the forms of organisms have been *created* by a human-like God, but describes their development in the sensory world strictly according to natural laws.

Meister Eckhart – as well as Johannes Tauler, Jacob Boehme, and Angelus Silesius – would feel profoundly at home contemplating natural science. *When understood properly*, one sees that the spirit of their worldview has evolved fully into this view of nature. They were not yet able to shine the light that had arisen within them upon the facts of nature itself, but this would no doubt have become their desire had natural science been available to them. They were unable to see nature in this light because no geology and no "natural history of Creation" narrated those processes to them. Only the Bible spoke in its own way of such processes.

Thus, to the best of their ability, they looked for spirit in the only place it may be found – in the human being's inner life. Today, they would have more and other means at their disposal than they did in their day to show that spirit, in a form manifest to the senses, can be found only in the human being. They would agree entirely with those who look for spirit, as a fact, not in the roots of nature but in its fruit. They would admit that the spirit in the sensory body is the *result of evolution* and that such spirit is not to be sought at earlier stages of evolution. They would understand that a "Creation-thought" [*Schöpfungsgedanke*] did not hold sway in the origination of spirit in an organism, just as surely as a "Creation-thought" did not cause apes to develop from marsupials.

In our time, people cannot speak of natural facts as Jacob Boehme did. But today there is also a viewpoint that brings Boehme's thinking closer to a worldview that includes modern science. It is not necessary to lose the spirit when one finds only what is natural in nature. Of course, today there are many who think that one must slip into a shallow, dry materialism by accepting at face value the "facts" discovered by the natural sciences. I stand completely upon the foundations of natural science. I am convinced that a view of nature like that of Ernst Haeckel becomes shallow only when people approach it with a world of shallow ideas. When I let the *revelations* of a "natural history of Creation" affect me, I feel something higher and more glorious than when I am confronted with the stories of supernatural miracles common to religious confessions. I know of nothing in "holy" books that reveals anything as sublime as the so-called dry fact that every human fetus rapidly progresses through a succession of all the forms through which its animal ancestors evolved.

Let us take to heart the magnificent facts that our senses perceive, and we will have little care for "miracles" foreign to the cycles of nature. If we experience spirit within ourselves, we do not need spirit in external nature. In my *Philosophy of Spiritual Activity*, I described my worldview, which does not believe it drives out spirit on account of viewing nature just as Darwin and Haeckel viewed it. A plant or an animal does not gain anything for me if I attribute to it a soul not perceived by my senses. I do not look for a "deeper," "spiritual" nature of things in the external world; I do not even assume it, because I believe that the knowledge illuminating my inner self protects me from doing so. I believe that things of the sensory world are as they appear to be because I see that true self-knowledge leads us to look only for natural processes in nature. I do not look for divine spirit in nature, because I believe I perceive the essence of human spirit in myself. I calmly acknowledge my animal ancestors, because I believe I recognize that no soul-like spirit *can be active* where these animal ancestors have their origins. I can only agree with Ernst Haeckel in his preference for the "eternal stillness of the grave" to the immortality of many religious doctrines (see Haeckel's *Riddle of the Universe*).[142] I consider it to be a degradation of the spirit, an abhorrent sin *against the spirit*, to conceive of a soul that continues to exist like a sensory being.

I hear a shrill dissonance when the facts of natural science according to Haeckel encounter the "piety" of many contemporary creeds. But I do not hear any of the spirit of the higher piety of Jacob Boehme and Angelus Silesius in a piety that harmonizes poorly with natural facts. The former harmonizes fully with the activity of the natural world. There is no contradiction in being permeated with the insights of modern science and at the same time embarking upon the path that Boehme and Silesius pursued in their search for the spiritual. Whoever takes this road in the way those thinkers did does not have to worry about slipping into shallow materialism, as long as he allows the secrets of nature to be told by a natural history of Creation. Whoever interprets my ideas in this sense will understand, in the same way as I, the last saying of the *Cherubinic Wanderer*, which will also sound the last note of this book.

Dear friend, this is enough for now. If you wish to read more, then go and become the writing and the essence yourself.[143, e]

[e] See addendum V, p. 172.

PREFACE TO THE 1924 EDITION

In this work, written more than twenty years ago, my intention was to answer the question: Why is it that a certain form of mysticism and the beginnings of contemporary natural-scientific thought confront one another during the thirteenth to the seventeenth centuries? I did not want to write a "history" of mysticism, but only to answer this question. Publications on this subject since the beginning of the twentieth century do not, in my opinion, provide any basis for altering anything in this attempt at an answer. This work can therefore appear again essentially unchanged.

The mystics discussed here were the last representatives of a means of inquiry and thinking that, in its specific nature, is foreign to contemporary consciousness. It is only the mood of soul living in this means of inquiry that is to be found in contemplative individuals of our time. The way of viewing natural phenomena with which those of this soul disposition, living before the time-period mentioned, were connected, has nearly disappeared. Modern natural science has taken its place.

The series of personalities described in this book were unable to carry that earlier method of inquiry into the future. It ceased to correspond to the forces of cognition that developed in European humanity from the thirteenth and fourteenth centuries on. What Paracelsus or Jacob Boehme preserved through this kind of research appears to us only as reminiscences of times past. In essence, all that remains to the contemplative person is the mood of soul. And in order to attain this mood, such people look for an impulse in the soul's own inclinations – whereas, in earlier times, this impulse lit up in the soul while observing nature. Some of those inclined toward mysticism today have no desire to enkindle mystical experiences through approaching what contemporary natural science teaches; rather, they desire to do so through what is contained in the works of that time-period here described. In this way, however, they alienate themselves from the most prominent concerns of the present time.

It might seem as though contemporary knowledge of nature, in its true form, fails to reveal a way for the soul to find the light of spirit through mystical contemplation. Why are mystically inclined souls satisfied with Meister Eckhart, Jacob Boehme, and others, but not with the book of nature, insofar as it today lies open to humankind through knowledge?

It is true that the way the book of nature is spoken of today certainly cannot lead to a mystical mood of soul.

The present work tries to show that this goes without saying. It attempts to do so by speaking of those spirits who, in the soul mood of old mysticism, developed a way of thinking that can also incorporate newer knowledge. This was the case, for example, with Nicholas of Cusa.

In such personalities, it becomes apparent that modern natural science, too, has a capacity for mystical deepening. For, a person such as Nicholas of Cusa would have been able to carry his thinking over into this science. In his time, one could have discarded the old means of inquiry while retaining the mystical disposition and adopting modern natural science, had it already existed.

But, whatever the human soul finds compatible with a way of inquiry, it must also be able to gain from it, if the soul is strong enough to do so.

I wanted to present the characteristic nature of medieval mysticism in order to show how it freed itself from its cultural roots (the ancient way of knowing), evolved into a form of independent mysticism, and yet cannot sustain itself because it lacks the mobility of soul it had earlier achieved through the quest for knowledge.

This leads to the thought that we must look for those elements in modern research that guide us toward mysticism. Through them, we can regain the mobility of soul that does not come to rest in a shadowy, sentimental mystical inner life, but rather strives upward toward spiritual understanding. Medieval mysticism withered because it lost its solid footing in the quest for knowledge that directs the forces of the soul upward toward the spirit. This book would encourage its readers to gain the forces leading toward the spiritual world through a proper understanding of the modern striving for knowledge.

Rudolf Steiner
Dornach, Switzerland, Autumn 1923

ADDENDA TO THE 1924 EDITION

Addendum I (p. 40): The fear of incurring an impoverishment of soul through an ascent to spirit is experienced only by those personalities who know spirit as but a collection of concepts removed from what the senses behold. Whoever raises himself, through spiritual seeing, to a life whose content surpasses the senses in terms of concreteness – such a person cannot have this fear. For it is only in abstractions that sensory existence grows pale; in "spiritual seeing," it appears in its true light for the first time, without losing anything of its sensory richness.

Addendum II (p. 84): In my writings, one will find "mysticism" spoken of in various ways. One will find the *seeming* contradiction – which some individuals wish to find in this – elucidated in the annotations to the new edition of my *Science of Knowing: Outline of an Epistemology Implicit in the Goethean Worldview*.[144]

Addendum III (p. 109): With a few words, I have here alluded to the path of spiritual cognition that I described in my later writings, especially in *Knowledge of the Higher Worlds: How Is It Achieved?*, *Occult Science: An Outline*, and *Riddles of the Soul*.[145]

Addendum IV (p. 145): These words should not be understood to suggest that it would be an aberration in our time to investigate the Bible and the spiritual world. They simply mean that a "Jacob Boehme of the nineteenth century" would be led to a "natural history of Creation" by paths similar to those that led him to the Bible in the sixteenth century. But from there he would press on toward the spiritual world.

Addendum V (p. 166): These final passages should not be misinterpreted as expressing a *non-spiritual* view of nature. Through them, I wanted only to strongly emphasize that the spirit that lies at the root of nature must be found *within* it, and should not be brought to it from outside. The rejection of "Creation-thoughts" makes reference to a form of "creating" similar to human creating, a creative activity that follows intentional thoughts. What is to be said about evolutionary history may be found in the preface to the new edition of my book *The Science of Knowing: Outline of an Epistemology Implicit in the Goethean Worldview.*

CITATION NOTES

All notes are provided by the editors of the German edition (Dornach: Rudolf Steiner Verlag, 1987) unless otherwise indicated. Notes by the editors of the Chadwick Library are designated "*Ed. 2017.*" Citation information that was originally provided in the body of the text by Rudolf Steiner is designated "*RS note.*"

[1] *Ed. 2017*: Rudolf Steiner, *The Philosophy of Spiritual Activity*, trans. W. Lindeman (Hudson, NY: Anthroposophic Press, 1986).

[2] *Ed. 2017*: This refers to the second part of *The Riddles of Philosophy* (Great Barrington, MA: SteinerBooks, 2009).

[3] A source could not be found for this and the following criticism of Rudolf Steiner.

[4] Ernst Haeckel, *Die Welträtsel. Gemeinverständliche Studien über monistische Philosophie* (Bonn, 1899). *Ed. 2017*: In English: *The Riddle of the Universe* (Buffalo, NY: Prometheus Books, 1992).

[5] G. W. F. Hegel, *Vorlesungen über die Geschichte der Philosophie*, vol. 3 (Berlin, 1844), pp. 95–96. *Ed. 2017*: In English: *Lectures on the History of Philosophy: Volume 3: Medieval and Modern Philosophy* (Lincoln, NE: University of Nebraska Press, 1995).

[6] *Ed. 2017*: *Erkenne dich selber.* Published as: Valentin Weigel, Collected Works, vol. 3: *Vom Gesetz oder Willen Gottes. Gnothi seauton* (Stuttgart: Frommann-Holzboog, 1996). Not available in English translation.

[7] Baruch Spinoza, *Ethik*, part 2, proposition 47. *Ed. 2017*: Full German title: *Die Ethik nach geometrischer Methode dargestellt* (Hamburg: Felix Meiner Verlag, 1976). In English: *Ethics*, trans. Samuel Shirley (Indianapolis, IN: Hackett Publishing Company, 1992).

[8] J. G. Fichte, *Einleitungvorlesungen in die Wissenschaftslehre, die transzendentale Logik und die Tatsachen des Bewußtseins*, vol. 9 of the complete works (Bonn, 1834), pp. 4–5. *Ed. 2017*: In English: *Introductions to the Wissenschaftslehre and Other Writings*, trans. Daniel Breazeale (Indianapolis, IN: Hackett Classics, 1994).

[9] This statement has only been found in Meister Eckhart's work. See: *Deutsche Mystiker des 14. Jahrhunderts, vol. 2: Meister Eckhart* [German mystics of the fourteenth century] (Leipzig, 1857), ed. Franz Pfeiffer, sermon 69, p. 220 [hereafter "Pfeiffer"]. See also: *Meister Eckhart, Deutsche Predigten und Traktate*, ed. and trans. Josef Quint (Munich: Hanser, 1963), sermon 36, p. 323 [hereafter "Quint"]. *Ed. 2017*: Franz Pfeiffer's compilation is available in English as *Works of Meister Eckhart* (Whitefish, MT: Kessinger Publishing, 2010), a reprint of Pfeiffer's original *Meister Eckhart*, trans. C. de B. Evans (London: John M. Watkins, 1924). Josef Quint's compilation is available in English as: *Meister Eckhart, Sermons and Treatises*, trans. Maurice O'C. Walshe, 3 vols. (Dorset, UK: Element Books, 1987, 1987, and 1991). These publications by Pfeiffer and Quint are the two principle sources for Eckhart's sermons, and will be referred to in the following notes.

[10] J. G. Fichte, *Grundlage der gesamten Wissenschaftslehre* (1794), note to §4. *Ed. 2017*: German Edition: (Hamburg: Felix Meiner Verlag, 1997). In English: Fichte, *The Science of Knowledge* (Cambridge, UK: Cambridge University Press, 1982).

[11] J. G. Fichte, *Einleitungvorlesungen in die Wissenschaftslehre*, p. 19. *Ed. 2017*: In English: *Introductions to the Wissenschaftslehre.*

[12] Ibid., p. 7.

[13] Emil Du Bois-Reymond, *Über die Grenzen des*

Naturerkennens (Leipzig, 1872). *Ed. 2017*: *The Limits of Our Knowledge of Nature*. In: *Popular Science Monthly*, vol. 5, May 1874, trans. J. Fitzgerald.

[14] Paul Asmus, *Das Ich und das Ding an sich* (Halle, 1873) [not available in English translation]. *RS note*: pp. 14–15.

[15] *Ed. 2017*: *The Philosophy of Spiritual Activity*, trans. W. Lindeman (op. cit.), chapter III, p. 38.

[16] Paul Asmus, *Die indogermanische Religion in den Hauptpunkten ihrer Entwicklung* (Halle, 1875) [not available in English translation]. *RS note*: vol. 1, p. 29.

[17] Spinoza, *Ethik*, part 5, proposition 25. *Ed. 2017*: In English: *Ethics*.

[18] Ibid., part 5, proposition 27.

[19] Letter from Humboldt to August Wilhelm Schlegel of June 21, 1823. *Briefwechsel zwischen W. v. Humboldt und A. W. Schlegel*, ed. Albert Leitzmann (Halle: Verlag von Max Niemeyer, 1908), pp. 157–63.

[20] The Bhagavad Gita, 15:7–10. *Ed. 2017*: This passage has been translated from the German version quoted by Rudolf Steiner (translator unknown). The decision to translate from the German serves to preserve the term "Inner Light," a term referenced elsewhere in the context of this introduction. For another modern English translation of this passage, see The Bhagavad Gita, trans. Eknath Easwaran (Tomales, CA: Nilgiri Press, 1985), pp. 220–21.

[21] Ibid., 18:17.

[22] Spinoza, *Ethik*, part 5, note to proposition 42. *Ed. 2017*: In English: *Ethics*.

[23] *Ed. 2017*: J. W. v. Goethe, *Maxims and Reflections* (London: Penguin, 1999), maxim 163. This trans. by W. Lindeman.

[24] Goethe, "Selige Sehnsucht" [Blessed longing] from the *West-östlichen Divan. Ed. 2017*: In English, cf. *Goethe's Collected Works, vol. 1: Selected Poems*, ed. Christopher Middleton (Princeton, NJ: Princeton University Press, 1994).

[25] Angelus Silesius, *Cherubinischer Wandersmann* (Stuttgart: Reclam, 1984), book 1, verses 8, 96. *Ed. 2017*: In English: *The Cherubinic Wanderer* (Mahwah, NJ: Paulist Press, 1986).

[26] Robert Hamerling, *Die Atomistik des Willens* (Hamburg, 1891) [not available in English translation]. *RS note*: vol. 2, pp. 213–14.

[27] Augustine, *Contra epistulam Manichaei quam vocant fundamenti*, 6. *Ed. 2017*: In English: Saint Augustine, *Against the Epistle of Manichaeus, Called Fundamental*, chapter 5: "Against the Title of the Epistle of Manichaeus" (Philip Schaff, 2011).

[28] *Ed. 2017*: 1 John 1, 3, King James Version (KJV).

[29] *Ed. 2017*: John 16:7, KJV.

[30] Meister Eckhart, *Von Abgescheidenheit* [On solitude]. In: Pfeiffer, pp. 491–92. *Ed. 2017*: In English: Pfeiffer, *Works of Meister Eckhart.*

[31] Not found in Pfeiffer. Quint: sermon 16, p. 227.

[32] Pfeiffer: sermon 65, p. 206. Quint: sermon 7, p. 186.

[33] Pfeiffer: sermon 13, p. 64. Quint: sermon 6, p. 178.

[34] Not found in Pfeiffer or Quint. An almost identical passage is found in Quint: sermon 7, p. 185.

[35] See Eckhart, *Von Abgescheidenheit* [On solitude]. In: Pfeiffer, p. 491. *Ed. 2017*: Romans 13:14, KJV.

[36] Meister Eckhart, *Vom Gottesreich* [On the kingdom of God]. See *Meister Eckharts Schriften und Predigten* [Meister Eckhart's writings and sermons], trans. and ed. H. Büttner (Jena, 1909), vol. 2, p. 209.

[37] Eckhart, *Von Abgescheidenheit* [On solitude]. In: Pfeiffer, p. 488.

[38] Ibid., p. 489.

[39] Pfeiffer: sermon 32, pp. 113–15. Quint: sermon 20, pp. 241–45.

[40] Pfeiffer: sermon 60, p. 193. Quint: sermon 34, p. 316.

[41] Source unknown.

[42] Pfeiffer: sermon 7, p. 38. Quint: sermon 35, p. 317.

[43] Pfeiffer: sermon 60, p. 192. Quint: sermon 34, p. 314.

[44] Pfeiffer: sermon 11, p. 60. Quint: sermon 49, p. 386.

[45] Pfeiffer: sermon 73, p. 231. Quint: sermon 33, p. 313.

[46] Pfeiffer: sermon 56, p. 181. Quint: sermon 26, p. 273.

[47] Source unknown.

[48] Pfeiffer: sermon 74, p. 232. Quint: sermon 29, p. 291.

[49] Source unknown.

[50] Pfeiffer: sermon 74, p. 232. Quint: sermon 29, p. 291.

[51] Ibid.

[52] Source unknown.

[53] Pfeiffer: sermon 59, pp. 189–90. Quint: sermon 25, p. 268.

[54] The quotations of Johannes Tauler used by Rudolf Steiner are from Julius Hamberger, *Johann Tauler's Predigten* [Johannes Tauler's sermons] (Frankfurt, 1864) [hereafter "Hamberger"]. Sermon 129, part III, p. 114.

[55] Hamberger: sermon 93, part II, pp. 225–26

[56] W. Preger, *Geschichte der deutschen Mystik* (Leipzig, 1881) [not available in English translation]. *RS note*: vol. 3, p. 161.

[57] Eckhart: Pfeiffer: sermon 96, p. 312. Quint: sermon 13, p. 216.

[58] Tauler: Hamberger: sermon 72, part II, p. 94.

[59] Hamberger: sermon 83, part II, p. 167.

[60] *Ed. 2017*: Preger, *Geschichte der deutschen Mystik. RS note*: vol. 3, pp. 219–20.

[61] Hamberger: sermon 15, part I, p. 113.

[62] Hamberger: sermon 45a, part I, p. 270.

[63] Source unknown.

[64] Hamberger: sermon 145, part III, pp. 190–91.

[65] *Das Buch des Meisters* [not available in English translation]. Available under the title: *Nicolaus von Basel, Bericht von der Bekehrung Taulers* [Nicholas of Basel, report on the conversion of Tauler], ed. Karl Schmidt (Strasbourg, 1875).

[66] In the final chapter of Karl Schmidt, ed., *Nicolaus von Basel*: "Meisterbuches" [The master book], p. 62.

[67] Heinrich Denifle, *Die Dichtungen des Gottesfreundes im Oberlande* (Berlin, 1880 and 1881) [not available in English translation].

[68] *Ed. 2017*: Preger, *Geschichte der deutschen Mystik.*

[69] *Ed. 2017*: None of these texts are available in English translation. The German titles are: *Von eime eiginwilligen weltwisen manne, der von eime heiligen weltpriestere gewiset wart uffe demuetige gehorsamme*, 1338; *Das Buch von den zwei Mannen*; *Der gefangene Ritter*, 1349; *Die geistliche Stege*, 1350; *Von der geistlichen Leiter*, 1357; *Das Meisterbuch*, 1369; *Geschichte von zwei jungen 15 jährigen Knaben. Ed. 1987*: All are contained in the charter book of the *Johanniterhaus* to the "*Grüne Wörth*" in Strasbourg, the so-called "Great German Memorial." Most are available in: Karl Schmidt, ed., *Nicolaus von Basel, Leben und ausgewählte Schriften* (Vienna, 1866). *Ed. 2017*: See also: Wilhelm Rath, *The Friend of God from the High Lands* (Stroud, UK: Hawthorn Press, 1991).

[70] Franz Pfeiffer, *Theologia deutsch* (Stuttgart, 1855). *Ed. 2017*: In English: *The Theologia Germanica of Martin Luther* (Mahwah, NJ: Paulist Press, 1980). Also known as *Theologia Germanica.*

[71] Pfeiffer, *Theologia deutsch*, chapter 3, pp. 11, 13.

[72] Ibid., chapter 2, pp. 7, 9.

[73] Ibid., chapter 1, pp. 3, 5, 7.

[74] *Ed. 2017*: i.e., *Theologia deutsch*, chapter 1.

[75] Ibid., chapter 2, p. 9.

[76] Ibid., chapter 7, p. 25.

[77] Ibid., chapter 15, pp. 51, 53.

[78] Ibid., chapter 24, p. 87.

[79] Ibid., chapter 54, p. 233.

[80] Heinrich Suso, *Lebensbeschreibung* [Life description], chapter 55, "Eine Ausrichtung: Wo und wie Gott ist" [Instruction concerning where God is and how God is]. In: *Heinrich Susos, genannt Amandus, Leben und Schriften*, ed. Melchior Diepenbrock (Regensburg, 1884), p. 292. *Ed. 2017*: In English, cf. *Henry Suso, The Exemplar: With Two German Sermons*, trans. Frank Tobin (Mahwah, NJ: Paulist Press, 1989).

[81] *Büchlein von der ewigen Weisheit.* In: H. Suso, *Lebensbeschreibung*, pp. 311–415. *Ed. 2017*: In English, cf. *Henry Suso, The Exemplar*, p. 205ff.

[82] H. Suso, *Büchlein von der ewigen Weisheit*, part one, chapter 5, p. 326.

[83] H. Suso, *Lebensbeschreibung*, chapter 55, p. 299.

[84] Tycho Brahe, *Opra omnia*, ed. L. L. Dreyer (Mauniae, 1929), pp. 220–21.

[85] K. Werner, *Franz Suarez und die Scholastik der letzten Jahrhunderte*, vol. 2 (Regensburg, 1861) [not available in English translation]. *RS note*: p. 122.

[86] Otto Willmann, *Geschichte des Idealismus* (Braunschweig, 1896) [not available in English translation]. *RS note*: vol. 2, 2nd ed., p. 396.

[87] *Ed. 2017*: *Geschichte des Idealismus. RS note*: p. 383.

[88] Joseph Kleutgen, *Die Theologie der Vorzeit* (Münster, 1867) [not available in English translation]; in the second, revised edition: p. 47. *RS note*: vol. 1, p. 39.

[89] "Visio sine comprehensione," in the writing titled *De apice theoriae* [On the summit of contemplation].

[90] In: *De docta ignorantia*, book III. Letter to Cardinal Julianus. *Ed. 2017*: In English: *Nicholas of Cusa on Learned Ignorance: A Translation and an Appraisal of De Docta Ignorantia*, trans. Jasper Hopkins (Minneapolis, MN: Arthur J. Banning Press, 1985).

[91] Hermann Helmholtz, *Die Tatsachen in der Wahrnehmung* (Berlin, 1879) [not available in English translation]. *RS note*: pp. 12–13.

[92] Erich Adikes, *Kant contra Haeckel* (Berlin, 1901), p. 120 [not available in English translation].

[93] An expression of Giordano Bruno, from "Abschiedsrede, welche Giordano Bruno vor den Professoren und Hörern auf der Akademie zu Wittenberg im Jahre 1588 am 8. März gehalten hat" [Farewell address held by Giordano Bruno before the professors and listeners of the academy in Wittenberg on March 8th, 1588]. In: Giordano Bruno, *Gesammelte Werke* (Jena, 1909), vol. 6, p. 86.

[94] Moriz Carrière, *Die philosophische Weltanschauung der Reformationszeit in ihren Beziehungen zur Gegenwart* [The philosophical worldview at the time of the Reformation in its relation to the present time] (Leipzig, 1887), p. 107ff.

[95] Available as: Wolfgang Ernst Heidel, *Johannes*

Trithemii Steganographia (Nürnberg, 1721).

[96] *Ed. 2017*: Henry Cornelius Agrippa, *Three Books of Occult Philosophy*, trans. J. Freake, ed. D. Tyson (St. Paul, MN: Llewellyn Worldwide, 1993).

[97] *Ed. 2017*: Henry Cornelius Agrippa, *Of the Vanitie and Uncertaintie of Artes and Sciences* (Northridge, CA: California State University, 1974).

[98] Franz Strunz, ed., *Paracelsus: Volumen Paramirum und Opus Paramirum* (Jena, 1904), book 1, chapter 1, p. 85. *Ed. 2017*: For selections in English, see: *Paracelsus: Essential Readings*, ed. Nicholas Goodrick-Clarke (Berkeley, CA: North Atlantic Books, 1999).

[99] P. R. Netzhammer, *Theophrastus Paracelsus: Das Wissenswerteste über dessen Leben, Lehre und Schriften* [Theophrastus Paracelsus: the most essential aspects of his life, teachings, and writings] (Einsiedeln, 1901), pp. 32–33. See also: R. Julius Hartmann, *Theophrast von Hohenheim* (Stuttgart and Berlin, 1904), pp. 30 and 80.

[100] Franz Strunz, ed., *Das Buch Paragranum* (Leipzig, 1903), p. 83. *Ed. 2017*: For selections in English, see: *Paracelsus: Essential Readings.*

[101] Ibid., p. 11.

[102] Netzhammer, *Theophrastus Paracelsus*, p. 85.

[103] Franz Strunz, ed., *Paracelsus: Opus Paramirum*, book 2, p. 172.

[104] Goethe, *Winckelmann*, I, "Antikes." This trans. W. Lindeman.

[105] Franz Strunz, ed., *Paracelsus: Opus Paramirum*, book 4, p. 279.

[106] Hans Kayser, *Vom Wesen der Dinge: Schriften Theophrasts von Hohenheim genannt Paracelsus* [On the essence of things: the writings of Theophrastus von Hohenheim, known as Paracelsus] (Leipzig, 1921), p. 299.

[107] Theophrastus Paracelsus, *Lebendiges Erbe* [Living heritage], ed. Jolan Jacobi (Zurich: Rascher Verlag, 1942), p. 242 (section VI: "Mensch und Schicksal" [The human being and destiny]).

[108] Carolus Linnaeus, *Genera plantarum* (Frankfurt, 1789), p. xii.

[109] Franz Strunz, ed., *Das Buch Paragranum*, p. 70.

[110] Ibid.

[111] Ibid., p. 86.

[112] Ibid., p. 70.

[113] *Ed. 2017*: *The Golden Grasp*, in: *Valentin Weigel: Selected Spiritual Writings*, ed. Andrew Weeks (Mahwah, NJ: Paulist Press, 2003). In German: *Der güldene Griff, das ist: All Ding ohne Irrthumb zu erkennen, vielen Hochgelährten unbekannt, und doch allen Menschen nothwendig zu wissen*; published in: Valentin Weigel: Collected Works, vol. 8: *Der Guldene Griff. Kontroverse Um Den Guldenen Griff. Vom Judicio Im Menschen: Im Auftrag Der Akademie Der Wissens* (Stuttgart: Frommann-Holzboog, 1997). *Know Thyself*: not available in English translation. In German: *Erkenne dich selber*; published in: Collected Works, vol. 3: *Vom Gesetz oder Willen Gottes. Gnothi seauton* (Stuttgart: Frommann-Holzboog, 1996). *On the Place of the World*, in: *Valentin Weigel: Selected Spiritual Writings*, p. 63ff. In German: *Vom Ort der Welt*; published in: Collected Works, vol. 10: *Vom Ort der Welt. Scholasterium christianum* (Stuttgart: Frommann-Holzboog, 2014).

[114] Jacob Boehme, *Apologia I contra Balthasar Tilken*, preface 25 and 26.

[115] Jacob Boehme, *Mysterium magnum*, chapter 9, no. 1.2; and *Die drei Prinzipien göttlichen Wesens*, chapter 7, no. 6. *Ed. 2017*: In English: *Mysterium Magnum*, 2 vols., trans. John Sparrow (London, 1772) (reprint: San Rafael, CA: Hermetica Press, 2007–2008); *Concerning*

the Three Principles of the Divine Essence: Of the Eternal, Dark, Light, and Temporary World, 2 vols., trans. John Sparrow, reissued by C. J. Barker (London: John M. Watkins, 1910) (reprint: Whitefish, MT: Kessinger Publishing, 2010).

[116] Source unknown, but the thought is found often throughout Jacob Boehme's work; for example, in: *Mysterium Magnum*, chapter 10, number 15; and 177 *Fragen von göttlicher Offenbarung* [177 questions on divine revelation (1624)], 3rd question, nos. 2–3.

[117] Jacob Boehme, *Anti-Stiefelius II*, 316.

[118] Jacob Boehme, *Apologia II contra Balthasar Tilken*, 140.

[119] Jacob Boehme, *Vom dreifachen Leben des Menschen*, chapter 4, no. 82 and chapter 5, no. 39. *Ed. 2017*: In English: *The Threefold Life of Man*, trans. John Sparrow (London, 1764, 1909) (reprint: Whitefish, MT: Kessinger Publishing, 2005).

[120] *Ed. 2017*: In English: Charles Lyell, *The Principles of Geology*, 3 vols. (Chicago: University of Chicago Press, 1990, 1991, 1992). Ernst Haeckel, *The History of Creation* (Ann Arbor, MI: University of Michigan Library, 2009); original German edition: *Natürliche Schöpfungsgeschichte* (Berlin, 1898).

[121] *Ed. 2017*: *The Coming of the Dawn*: published in English as: *The Aurora*, trans. John Sparrow (1656; London, 1764) (reprint: Whitefish, MT: Kessinger Publishing, 2010); *Concerning the Three Principles of the Divine Essence* (op. cit.); *The Threefold Life of Man* (op. cit.); *The Eye Turned upon Itself*: not available in English translation; in German: *Das umgewandt Auge*, published in: *Jakob Böhme's Sämtliche Werke, vol. 6* (reprint: London: Forgotten Books, 2017); *Signatura Rerum or the Signature of All Things* (London, 1651) (reprint: Whitefish, MT:

Kessinger Publishing, 2010); *Mysterium Magnum* (op. cit.).

[122] *RS note*: *Anthropologie* (Leipzig 1888), p. 528. *Ed. 2017*: In English: Paul Topinard, *Anthropology* (Ithaca, NY: Cornell University Library, 2009).

[123] *Ed. 2017*: John 4:24, KJV.

[124] Ernst Haeckel, *Die Welträtsel*, p. 333. *Ed. 2017*: In English: *The Riddle of the Universe.*

[125] B. Carneri, *Empfindung und Bewusstsein* (Bonn, 1893) [not available in English translation]. *RS note*: p. 15.

[126] Giordano Bruno, *Von der Ursache, dem Prinzip und dem Einen. Ed. 2017*: German edition: (Hamburg: Felix Meiner Verlag, 2007). In English: *Cause, Principle and Unity: And Essays on Magic* (Cambridge, UK: Cambridge University Press, 1998).

[127] Ibid., second dialog; statement of Theophilo.

[128] Ibid., statement of Theophilio.

[129] Franz Brentano, *Die vier Phasen der Philosophie und ihr augenblicklicher Stand* [The four phases of philosophy and their present state] (Stuttgart, 1895), p. 20.

[130] Angelus Silesius, *Cherubinischer Wandersmann* (op. cit.), book 1: 11, 14, 18, 80, 81, 82. *Ed. 2017*: In English: *The Cherubinic Wanderer* (op. cit.).

[131] Ibid., book 2: 85; book 4: 10; book 1: 140.

[132] Ibid., book 1: 12, 13, 108; book 2: 183; book 4: 215, 224.

[133] Ibid., book 4: 56; 5: 88, 126.

[134] Ibid., book 2: 178.

[135] Ibid., book 1: 96, 8.

[136] Ibid., book 4: 160, 161.

[137] Ibid., book 1: 118, 98.

[138] Ibid., book 5: 277.

[139] Ibid., book 1: 288, 289.

[140] Ibid., book 3: 98; book 5: 193.

[141] *Ed. 2017*: *Goethe's Worldview*, trans. W. Lindeman (Spring Valley, NY: Mercury Press, 1985).

[142] *RS note*: Ernst Haeckel, *Die Welträtsel*, p. 239. *Ed. 2017*: In English: *The Riddle of the Universe.*

[143] Angelus Silesius, *Cherubinischer Wandersmann*, book 6: 263. *Ed. 2017*: In English: *The Cherubinic Wanderer.*

[144] *Ed. 2017*: Rudolf Steiner, *The Science of Knowing*, trans. W. Lindeman (Spring Valley, NY: Mercury Press, 1988), p. 127.

[145] *Ed. 2017*: Rudolf Steiner, *Knowledge of the Higher Worlds: How Is It Achieved?*, trans. D. S. Osmond and C. Davy (London: Rudolf Steiner Press, 1993). *Occult Science: An Outline*, trans. G. and M. Adams (London: Rudolf Steiner Press, 1979). *Riddles of the Soul*, trans. W. Lindeman (Spring Valley, NY: Mercury Press, 1996); selections of *Riddles of the Soul* are also published under the title *The Case for Anthroposophy*, trans. O. Barfield (Oxford: Barfield Press, 2010).

TWO PUBLISHER'S NOTES

ON THE SELECTION OF RUDOLF STEINER'S WRITTEN WORKS

A small group, inspired by the work of the late horticulturalist Alan Chadwick, initiated the idea to republish – mostly in new or thoroughly revised English translations – a number of the written works of Rudolf Steiner.

The unifying theme of this edition is that, to this small group, these texts speak most directly of Dr. Steiner.

ON THE APPROACH TO TRANSLATION AND THE GENDER NEUTRAL QUESTION

Rudolf Steiner generally refers to the individual human being ("der Mensch") in the third person singular form; such references in German are traditionally translated into English using the pronouns "he/his." For a translator preferring an alternative, the pronoun "one," or the phrase "he or she" is an option; but in texts where reflexive references often occur many times within a single sentence, consistently using "one," or "he or she," can present a challenge to the fidelity of the author's intended rhythm or syntax.

An alternative "gender neutral" approach is to replace references to the individual with references to the collective whole (of all human beings). Thus, "he/his" becomes "we/our" or "they/their."

Here, gender neutrality is upheld, but, again, at the expense of the author's chosen form, and more specific identification with "the individual."

The editorial board of the Chadwick Library recognizes that compromise is inherent in each possibility. The editorial board is equally of the view that in some instances the author's direct address to the individual is of a heightened necessity, while in others, a reference to the collective could just as well suffice. We have attempted to find a balance, while at the same time allowing for judgment and freedom for each of the translators.

As was common in his time, Rudolf Steiner used the third person singular grammatical form "he/his" as a neutral term. The pronoun "he/his" was intended, and regularly used, as an expression of neither masculine nor feminine determination; it was understood that grammatical "genus" does not equal gender – as is still widely sensed to be true in the German language today.

This is the third volume to be published in the Chadwick Library Edition of Selected Written Works of Rudolf Steiner. The translation was originally made by Karl E. Zimmer, and the revision is by Jon McAlice and Thomas O'Keefe.
Design by Martino Mardersteig in Caslon MM version, setting and printing by Opero in Verona, on Munken Pure paper. Binding by Ruggero Rigoldi in Monza.
Of a total of 850 copies, 750 copies have been bound with leather spines, and 100 have been bound in full leather and numbered 1 to 100.

VOLUMES PUBLISHED TO DATE

Vol. 1 The Case for Anthroposophy
Vol. 2 Goethean Science: Introductions to Goethe's Natural-Scientific Writings
Vol. 3 Mystics at the Dawn of the Modern Age and Their Relation to the Current Natural-Scientific Paradigm

FORTHCOMING VOLUMES

The Riddles of Philosophy (two volumes)
A Path to Self-Knowledge
Christianity as Mystical Fact and the Mysteries of Antiquity
The Threshold of the Spiritual World
How Does One Attain Cognitions of the Higher Worlds?
Theosophy
An Outline of Esoteric Science (three volumes)